CREATIVE
NATURAL
COOKING

Priscilla Gove Heininger

Ruth Knighton Malinowski

WEATHERVANE
BOOKS

About the Authors

Priscilla Gove Heininger, a native Vermonter, is married and has three children. She is a home economist with a wide range of experience in nutrition, home gardening, and natural foods.

Ruth Knighton Malinowski teaches food and nutrition at the University of Maryland and is a nutrition consultant for the school lunch program. She has authored several cookbooks.

Acknowledgment

We wish to thank our husbands and families for their helpful suggestions and endless patience in tasting these recipes.

contents

introduction

Recently the term "natural foods" has appeared everywhere. To the consumer this term often means confusion. What is "natural"? Is anything natural anymore?

Some people define natural foods as foods grown only organically, without the use of chemical fertilizers. To others natural is the basic food containing no additives or preservatives; that is, in its natural state, but without specific references as to the method by which it is grown. We feel that preferences in origin of foods depend on an individual's values.

Since the term "natural" may include everything from prepared mixes with no chemical additives to foods grown and preserved in a home garden, our definition will draw from both sides, with emphasis on "back to the basics," or the methods of cooking "from scratch" that our grandmothers used. Our goal is to present a variety of delicious, nutritious additive-free recipes that can be prepared from basic, easily found ingredients. Sometimes these basic ingredients may include the conveniences of canned or frozen foods, because today's cook may not always find it possible to grow and preserve the entire food supply. However, basic may include the choice of mixing and baking your own graham crackers from scratch. By including a wide variety of recipes, this book will provide the chance to try both practical and fun recipes using basic ingredients.

basic ingredients

Basic ingredients in natural-foods cooking include as many unprocessed foods as possible. Whole grains, unrefined flours, beans, nuts, and seeds play an important role. Emphasis is on using fewer highly refined ingredients, such as white sugar, and placing the focus on the "straight from nature" alternative, such as honey. The use of sugar, also, is kept to a minimum with preference on fresh or dried fruits as the dietary source of this.

Many ingredients for cooking naturally may be found in local supermarkets. Some, however, are not and must be purchased at specialty food stores or through food cooperatives. As you acquire a taste for certain foods and learn to incorporate them into your daily eating patterns, joining a local food co-op, if one exists in your area, can be very beneficial.

If natural cooking is a new experience for you, begin gradually. The taste of whole grains, or the "real" flavor instead of an artificial one, will be noticeable in your meals. Children, especially, should be introduced to whole grains and unfamiliar foods over a period of time. Start by adding small proportions of whole grains to what you now cook, then wait until the flavor becomes familiar before adding more. Be patient! To help develop this taste, we have included recipes with both unbleached and whole-grain flours.

The principles for serving nutritious meals are the same in using natural foods as in any type of cooking. The "Basic Four" food groups, as developed by the United States Department of Agriculture, provide a guide in planning nutritious meals. For adults these include two servings of milk or milk products; four servings of fruits and vegetables; two or more servings of meat, poultry, fish, or eggs; and four or more servings of enriched or whole-grain breads and cereals each day. Included in the fruit and vegetable group is one serving of citrus fruit or other good source of ascorbic acid (vitamin C) each day and one serving of a dark green, yellow, or orange vegetable every other day as a source of vitamin A. Since the Basic Four food groups cover practically every food available, it is important to vary one's choice of foods each day within each group. The greater the variety of foods eaten within a diet, the more chance there is of providing adequate amounts of trace elements. The body is a delicate balance of chemical interactions that depend on the presence of many different food elements at one time in order to work together. Including as much variety as possible in food selections and using the Basic Four as a guideline for these choices assures allowing the necessary nutrients to work together in providing good health.

As you explore the world of eating naturally, you will become aware of the variety of foods available and choices that we cannot begin to cover in one book. As you experience new recipes and acquire tastes for whole grains and "old-fashioned" cooking, we hope that you and your family will become "spoiled," knowing how good foods can really taste. Package mixes may have their merits, but they can never replace basic "from-scratch" cooking! In turning to natural foods and nutritious additive-free recipes that are prepared from basic ingredients, you are better able to know exactly what you are eating because you have put those ingredients there yourself. We hope you will enjoy the opportunity to try some of our favorite natural-food recipes.

special ingredients

Here is a brief explanation of some of the ingredients used in the recipes in this book and natural-foods cooking in general:

unbleached flour

Although unbleached or all-purpose flour is not as popular as whole-grain flours in natural-foods cookery, we have included it in some recipes. There are times when taste, texture, or finished product merit its use. In choosing all-purpose or unbleached flour, always use enriched flour to which some of the key nutrients have been returned. Unbleached flour has the advantage of being less refined than bleached white all-purpose flour and is high in the necessary gluten for bread-making.

whole-wheat pastry flour

This whole-wheat flour is a boon to the homemaker who loves to bake. It is ground from soft wheat and is lower than regular whole-wheat flour in gluten. As its name implies, it is excellent for baking pastries, quick breads, cakes, and cookies, because it gives the product a tender, flaky crust. It can replace unbleached or all-purpose white flour cup for cup in most recipes, with similar product results. Whole-wheat pastry flour can be used in all baked goods except yeast breads, which depend on a higher gluten content for their structure. It can be purchased at specialty stores or most food co-ops. Many of our baked-goods recipes call for whole-wheat pastry flour. If it is not available, substitute all-purpose flour, cup for cup. Whole-wheat flour also can be used; this substitution is described below.

whole-wheat flour

Thought of as the "staff of life," whole-wheat flour is the flour "Gramma" used. It is ground from hard winter wheat and can be used in all baked goods. The resulting product will be heavier than that made with unbleached flour. If you do not use whole-wheat flour regularly, change your baking habits to it step by step as you discover your own likes and dislikes. If whole-wheat flour is sifted, it may be substituted cup for cup for whole-wheat pastry flour; otherwise use only 7/8 cup of whole-wheat flour for each cup of pastry or all-purpose flour. To prevent rancidity, both whole-wheat pastry flour and whole-wheat flour should be stored in a cool place, such as a refrigerator or freezer.

triticale flour

Triticale is a new grain that was originally a cross between wheat and rye. Triticale flour contains a high protein content but is low in gluten, so it must be used in combination with other flours in baking, much the same as rye flour. It has a sweet, nutty flavor and, when used in correct proportions with other flours, produces a nutritious, tasty product.

other specialty flours

These flours include rye, buckwheat, oat, rice, soybean, and cornmeal. Each produces its own characteristic flavor when added to baked products. This type of flour is usually combined with unbleached or whole-wheat flour because, alone, the resulting product would be heavy and unacceptable by modern baking standards.

whole grains

Soaked and cooked until tender, whole grains are then eaten as cereals or added to other dishes. Some, such as brown rice and barley, make delicious casserole extenders as well as complementing other foods. Also, whole grains may be sprouted or purchased as flakes, such as rolled oats and wheat flakes, and added to baked goods. In flake form they make delicious granola-type cereals. Whole grains are also ground and used as flour. All forms of whole grains should be stored at a cool temperature.

dried peas and beans

These protein extenders come in a seemingly endless variety. There are black, red, white, mung, navy, soldier, yellow-eye, lima, soy, aduki, and other beans. Your familiarity will probably be reflected by the tastes and popularity of those available in your region. Likewise, members of the pea family are available in various kinds, such as whole dried peas, split peas (yellow and green), garbanzos, and lentils.

Legumes, when combined with other sources of protein, work together to provide complete protein. Cooked, they are used in soups, salads, and casseroles. Uncooked, they may be sprouted and served in salads, sandwiches, or main dishes.

Generally, to cook dried peas or beans, wash, then soak them overnight in twice as much water as beans. In the morning bring the same water and beans to a boil, then lower the heat and simmer until tender. A shorter method for tenderizing beans is to cover beans with cold water, bring them to a boil, and simmer them for 5 minutes. Remove the beans from heat, cover tightly, and let them stand for 1 hour. This takes the place of soaking beans overnight. Proceed to cook beans until tender, according to package or recipe directions. The amount of cooking time required varies with each type of bean. Most beans double in volume with soaking and cooking, although some, such as soybeans, will expand three times.

sprouts

Popular types of sprouting seeds include alfalfa, clover, mung bean, fenugreek, radish, chia, sesame, flax, and lentil. Try sprouting grains, such as wheat or rye, or other vegetable and herb seeds for variety. The list is practically endless! Choose only seeds that are labeled especially for sprouting. They may be purchased at specialty food stores. *Do not sprout seeds purchased for gardening or sold to be grown,* as many have been treated with pesticides or dyes and can be harmful if eaten. Check with your state extension service if you have questions about types to try or origins of the seeds.

When sprouting seeds, darkness and a room temperature of 65 to 70°F are best. Warmer temperatures promote mold growth. See "Starting Sprouts" (see Index) for a specific method.

When are the sprouts ready to eat? Smaller seeds, such as alfalfa, may be grown up to 1 inch long, but some larger varieties are best when only ¼ to ½ inch long. Taste and experiment to know what you prefer.

Imagination is the key to using sprouts. Eaten alone as snacks, they are nutritious and delicious. Sprouts, especially alfalfa sprouts, substitute for lettuce in sandwiches and have the same advantage of staying crisp and crunchy. For this same reason, sprouts are excellent salad additions. Try adding them to soups, vegetables, and breads. Be creative and enjoy sprouts!

nuts and seeds

Nuts and seeds are added to foods for their nutritional value, flavor, and texture. Nuts are served as snacks or ground into nut butters. In natural-foods cooking, both nuts and seeds are welcome additions to cookies, vegetables, salads, and granolas, since they are an added source of protein, vitamins, and minerals. Because of the high fat content, shelled nuts should be refrigerated or frozen to prolong freshness. Seeds may be kept in a cool, dry place.

fruits and vegetables

Natural-foods cookery takes advantage of the important nutrients that fresh fruits and vegetables contribute to the diet. The key to using vegetables lies in freshness and in eating them either raw or crisp-cooked, in order to preserve as many vitamins as possible.

Fruits, naturally sweet, contribute a healthy replacement for candy. They make good snacks and desserts as well as adding color and flavor to main dishes. Many kinds of dried fruits are available and play an important role in natural dishes. Also, these serve as nutritious snacks by themselves or in combination with nuts and seeds.

oils and butter

Much has been written about kinds of fats. Although fats in the American diet have gained a bad reputation, a certain amount is necessary for both energy and utilization of fat-soluble vitamins. The controversy lies in the types of fats eaten—animal versus vegetable, saturated versus unsaturated, and liquid versus solid.

Our main concern relative to natural foods is in simplicity. Therefore, butter is specified in most recipes because it is less refined and contains the least number of additives. If you have a problem with cholesterol, substitute a lightly polyunsaturated margarine for butter. In recipes calling for vegetable oil, we recommend safflower oil because it is the most polyunsaturated oil. Preferences and availability will determine your choice of oils.

Unrefined or cold-pressed oils are perferred in natural cooking by some persons because they have been subjected to less processing. Refrigerate unprocessed oils to prevent rancidity.

sweeteners

Preference is given to honey, maple syrup, molasses, and brown sugar as sweeteners because they contain trace elements, as opposed to refined (cane) sugar which supplies only "empty calories."

It is generally recognized that all sugars play too large a role in the American diet and should be limited. As a person begins to cut down sugar intake, "taste" for sweets decreases. (The process is also reversible!) Although fruits, both dried and fresh, provide a natural sweet touch at the end of a meal, there are times when we all love other types of sweet desserts. For this reason, cookies, cakes, and other desserts are included in this book with the hope that they will be eaten wisely and will not replace other nutritious foods in meals. In these desserts sugar has been kept to a minimum and other nutritious ingredients have been included so that they will provide some good nutrition at the same time.

yeast

The yeast in these recipes is measured both by specific amount, such as 1 tablespoon, and by the number of packages. The reasons for this are that active dry yeast obtained at the grocery store in individual packets contains a preservative and is expensive, particularly if you bake a lot. By contrast, active dry yeast granules, which can be purchased by the pound (or part of a pound) at specialty food stores, have no added preservatives and cost less per ounce. A scant tablespoon of these active dry yeast granules is equal to one ¼-ounce package of dry yeast. Active dry yeast granules can be dissolved in warm water and used the same as any dry yeast, except where the yeast is first combined with flour. In those recipes, whirl dry granules in a blender before combining them with flour, to assure a more uniform distribution.

Dry-yeast granules should be stored in an airtight container in a cool, dry atmosphere for up to six months, or frozen for longer storage. For the busy cook, a jar of yeast granules stored in a freezer door within easy reach is particularly handy. The frozen yeast granules can be measured out when needed and, if not used regularly, will still remain active.

appetizers

avocado cheese appetizers

Yield: 32 appetizers

  1⅓ cups shredded cheddar cheese
  10 slices bacon, cooked crisp, crumbled
  2 tablespoons minced fresh onion
  2 teaspoons soy sauce
  ¾ teaspoon lemon juice
  2 ripe avocados, peeled, seeds removed
  Salt and pepper to taste
  English-muffin halves

Combine cheese, bacon, onion, soy sauce, and lemon juice.

Mash avocados with fork until smooth. Add cheese mixture. Salt and pepper to taste.

Toast English-muffin halves. Spread with avocado mixture. Cut each muffin half into 4 to 5 wedges. Place on baking sheet. Broil just until bubbly and cheese has melted. Serve immediately.

soft cheese spread

A cooking thermometer and cheesecloth are essential for preparing this recipe.

Yield: 1 cup

   2 quarts skim milk
   2 cups buttermilk
   1 teaspoon salt
   1 teaspoon black pepper
   1 tablespoon coarsely ground black pepper

In large saucepan heat skim milk and buttermilk to 170°F. Stir occasionally to prevent scorching. Maintain temperature between 170 and 175°F until curds form in milk, about 30 minutes or more.

Meanwhile dampen 1 yard cheesecloth; fold in thirds. Line colander with cheesecloth. Using slotted spoon, place curds in colander to drain. Discard remaining liquid (the whey). Drain curds about 1 hour.

Mash curds to remove additional water. Scrape cheese from cheesecloth into bowl. Mix in salt and regular pepper. Form 2 or more balls or other shapes with cheese; sprinkle surfaces with coarse black pepper.

Serve spread with crackers or toast.

brie crackers

Yield: About 5 dozen

   ½ cup butter or margarine, softened
   8 ounces Brie cheese, room temperature
   ½ cup all-purpose flour
   ½ cup whole-wheat flour
   ⅛ teaspoon cayenne pepper
   ¼ teaspoon salt
   ½ cup sesame seeds

Beat all ingredients except sesame seeds in medium-size bowl. Divide mixture in half; form each half into long round roll. Wrap waxed paper around each roll; refrigerate at least 12 hours.

Slice chilled rolls into ¼-inch rounds. Sprinkle with sesame seeds. Place on cookie sheets. Bake at 400°F 12 minutes. Cool; store in tightly covered container.

swiss-cheese squares

swiss-cheese squares

Yield: 1½ dozen

   2 cups all-purpose flour
   2½ teaspoons baking powder
   ½ teaspoon baking soda
   1 teaspoon salt
   ⅓ cup shortening
   ½ cup buttermilk
   1 cup grated Swiss cheese (4 ounces)
   1 egg, beaten
   2 tablespoons poppy seeds

Sift flour, baking powder, baking soda, and salt. Cut in shortening with pastry blender or 2 knives until mixture resembles dry cornmeal. Add enough milk to form soft dough that cleans side of bowl. Knead cheese into dough 1 to 2 minutes. Roll dough to ½ inch thick. Cut into squares, using scalloped knife or pizza cutter. Brush tops with egg; sprinkle with poppy seeds. Place on ungreased cookie sheet. Bake in preheated 450°F oven 10 minutes or until golden brown. Best when served hot.

seafood cocktail

Yield: 4 servings

> 1 orange
> 16 blue grapes, some halved and seeded
> Bibb lettuce leaves
> 1 8-ounce can white or green asparagus tips
> 12 ounces canned or cooked seafood (crab, shrimp, lobster, etc.,
>   thoroughly chilled)
> Cooked crab claws for garnish
> Unpeeled orange slices for garnish

cocktail dressing

> ¼ cup mayonnaise
> ¼ cup plain yogurt
> 1 teaspoon catsup
> 1 teaspoon prepared horseradish
> 2 teaspoons lemon juice
> Salt and pepper to taste

Cut peel from orange; remove white membrane. Slice orange; cut each slice into quarters.

Line cocktail glasses with lettuce. Arrange orange pieces, grape halves, and asparagus on lettuce. Place seafood on top.

Blend together all dressing ingredients. Pour about 2 tablespoons dressing over top of each cocktail. Garnish each with half slice of orange, whole grapes, and crab claw. Serve at once.

seafood cocktail

stuffed pepper slices

Yield: 4 to 6 servings

1 red pepper
1 green pepper
8 ounces cottage cheese
2 tablespoons milk
1 tablespoon chopped pimiento
1 tablespoon chopped parsley
1 tablespoon chopped watercress
1 tablespoon chopped chives
¼ teaspoon salt
⅛ teaspoon white pepper
1 teaspoon lemon juice
1 envelope (1 tablespoon) unflavored gelatin
⅓ cup cold water
Lettuce leaves

stuffed pepper slices

Cut tops off peppers. Remove seeds; wash.
Cream cottage cheese in blender (thin with milk if necessary); remove. Add pimiento, parsley, watercress, chives, salt, pepper, and lemon juice.
Soak gelatin in cold water; dissolve completely over simmering water. Add to cheese mixture. Fill peppers with mixture; chill in refrigerator at least 2 hours.
Cut each pepper into 4 thick slices. Serve on lettuce.

stuffed mushrooms

Yield: 6 to 8 servings

1 pound mushrooms (caps 2 to 3 inches in diameter)
4 tablespoons butter or margarine, melted
3 tablespoons finely chopped onions
1 tablespoon butter
2 tablespoons Madeira
¼ cup fine dry bread crumbs
¼ cup grated Swiss cheese
¼ cup grated Parmesan cheese
4 tablespoons minced fresh parsley
½ teaspoon tarragon
¼ teaspoon pepper
2 tablespoons heavy cream

Remove stems from mushrooms. Brush caps with 2 tablespoons melted butter. Place hollow-side-up in roasting pan.

Mince mushroom stems; squeeze in towel to remove moisture.

Sauté onions in 1 tablespoon butter to soften. Add mushroom stems; cook over high heat, stirring frequently, about 5 minutes or until most moisture has disappeared. Add Madeira; boil until mostly evaporated. Remove from heat. Mix in bread crumbs, cheeses, parsley, tarragon, and pepper. Bind together with cream. Fill mushroom caps with stuffing. (Mushrooms can be prepared ahead to this point. Refrigerate until ready to use.)

Just before baking, top with drops of melted butter. Bake in preheated 375°F oven 15 minutes or until caps are tender and stuffing slightly browned.

soups

asparagus soup

Yield: 6 servings

30 stalks asparagus (about 2 pounds)
4 quarts water
1 tablespoon salt
¼ cup minced onion
¼ cup minced parsley
1 teaspoon ground coriander
2 tablespoons butter or margarine
1 tablespoon flour
2 cups chicken broth, heated
½ cup light (table) cream
1 tablespoon lemon juice
½ teaspoon salt
¼ teaspoon white pepper

Peel asparagus with potato peeler; trim tough ends. Tie together in 3 bunches; simmer in large pot of salted water until just tender. Lift out bundles; place in sink of cold water. When cool, drain on paper towels. Cut tips from stalks; reserve. Cut stalks into 1-inch pieces; reserve.

Sauté onion and parsley with coriander and butter in medium saucepan until vegetables are softened. Stir in flour; cook 3 minutes. Remove pan from heat. Stir in broth; simmer 5 minutes. Add asparagus stalks.

Puree mixture in blender or food mill until smooth. Do this by batches. Return puree to saucepan; stir in cream and asparagus tips; heat through. Stir in lemon juice. Add salt and pepper; adjust seasonings to taste. Serve soup hot or chilled.

hearty barley soup

Yield: 4 to 6 main-dish servings

  1 pound lean ground beef
  1 large onion, finely chopped
  1 cup chopped celery
  1 cup finely chopped cabbage or fresh broccoli stems
  ½ cup barley
  3½ cups beef stock or bouillon
  ½ cup tomato sauce
  ½ teaspoon salt
  ⅛ teaspoon pepper
  ¼ teaspoon ground marjoram
  1 bay leaf
  Dash of chili powder

Brown beef and onion in large saucepan or Dutch oven. Pour off excess fat. Add celery, cabbage, and barley; stir-fry 3 to 5 minutes. Stir in remaining ingredients; simmer, covered, 1 hour or until barley is tender.

garbanzo bean soup

Yield: 3½ quarts

  1 pound garbanzo beans (chick-peas)
  1 teaspoon salt
  Water to cover
  2 quarts water
  1 meaty ham bone
  3 beef bouillon cubes
  10 slices bacon, diced (6 ounces)
  2 medium onions, chopped
  2 medium potaotes, peeled, diced
  1 tablespoon salt
  Pinch of saffron
  1 pound kielbasa sausage, cut into thin slices

Soak garbanzos overnight in salted water to cover beans.
  Drain beans; place in Dutch oven. Add 2 quarts water, ham bone, and bouillon cubes; cook over low heat 45 minutes.
  Sauté bacon and onion together until golden brown. Remove from pan with slotted spoon. Add to bean mixture, along with potatoes, salt, and saffron. Cook 45 to 50 minutes, until potatoes are tender. Add kielbasa; cook 20 to 30 minutes. Remove ham bone. Serve.

lentil soup

Yield: 3 quarts

> 1 pound dried lentils
> 6 slices bacon, diced
> 1 cup chopped onion
> ½ cup chopped carrots
> 6 cups water
> 1½ teaspoons salt
> ½ teaspoon pepper
> ½ teaspoon thyme
> 2 bay leaves
> ½ cup grated potato
> 1 ham bone or 2 smoked pork hocks
> 2 tablespoons fresh lemon juice

Wash and sort lentils. Soak overnight, or bring to boil; boil 2 minutes. Cover; let stand 1 hour. Drain.

Sauté bacon in 4- or 5-quart Dutch oven until crisp; remove.

Sauté onion and carrots in bacon grease until onion is golden. Add lentils, water, seasonings, potato, and ham bone; simmer, covered, 3 hours. (Or cook in slow cooker on low 6 hours.)

To serve, remove bay leaves and ham bone; skim fat. Remove meat from ham bone. Mash lentils slightly to thicken soup. Stir in lemon juice just before serving.

cream of broccoli soup

Yield: 5 cups

> 3 cups diced fresh broccoli stems (or 2 packages frozen chopped broccoli)
> 1 small onion, chopped
> 1 cup chicken broth or bouillon
> 2 tablespoons butter or margarine
> 1 tablespoon all-purpose flour
> 1½ teaspoons salt
> ⅛ teaspoon nutmeg
> Pepper to taste
> 1 cup light (table) cream

Bring broccoli, onion, and broth to boil in medium saucepan. Simmer 10 to 12 minutes, until vegetables are tender. Transfer to blender; blend smooth, blending only ½ of hot mixture at a time.

Melt butter in saucepan. Add flour, salt, nutmeg, and pepper; stir smooth. Blend in cream and broccoli mixture. Cook, stirring, over medium heat until almost boiling. Adjust salt if desired. Remove from heat. Serve immediately.

cheese–vegetable soup

Yield: 6 servings

½ cup chopped carrot
½ cup chopped onion
½ cup chopped celery
2 cups chicken broth
2 slices bacon
1 tablespoon butter or margarine
⅓ cup flour

1½ cups milk
8 ounces sharp cheddar cheese, shredded
½ cup light (table) cream
½ teaspoon salt
⅛ teaspoon white pepper
1 sprig parsley, chopped

Add vegetables to broth in medium saucepan; simmer, covered, until tender.

Meanwhile sauté bacon in butter until crisp. Drain on paper towels; reserve.

Blend flour into remaining fat; cook 1 to 2 minutes (mixture should be thick and bubbling). Slowly blend in milk. Cook and stir until smooth and thickened. Add cheese; heat until melted.

Place hot vegetable–broth mixture in blender; puree. Add to hot cheese mixture. Stir in cream and seasonings. Heat to just below boiling.

Garnish with crumbled bacon and parsley. Serve soup hot.

gazpacho

gazpacho

Yield: 4 servings

4 medium tomatoes, peeled, chopped
1 small onion, chopped
1 green pepper, seeded, chopped
⅛ teaspoon garlic powder
2 tablespoons lemon juice
½ teaspoon salt
Dash of freshly ground pepper
Sliced cucumbers
Chopped onions
Croutons

Puree tomatoes, onion, and green pepper in blender. Add garlic powder, lemon juice, salt, and pepper.

Serve gazpacho chilled with garnishes of cucumber slices, chopped onions, and croutons, or serve side dishes of finely chopped tomatoes, onions, and green pepper.

hot potato soup

Yield: 5 cups

    2 tablespoons butter or margarine
    1½ cups thinly sliced onions
    2 tablespoons minced celery leaves
    3 cups chicken broth
    2 cups diced peeled potatoes
    1¼ teaspoons salt
    ¼ cup light (table) cream
    Parsley, chopped

Melt butter in large saucepan. Fry onions and celery slowly until onions are soft but not brown. Add broth, potatoes, and salt. Simmer, covered, until potatoes are very tender, about 1 hour.

Blend hot mixture in blender, small amount at a time. Return to saucepan. Add cream. Taste; add more salt if needed. Warm again, just until steamy.

Ladle soup into bowls; garnish with parsley.

squash soup

Yield: 8 servings

    1 large winter squash (about 2 pounds)
    1 cup water
    1 teaspoon salt
    ½ cup chopped onion
    1 tablespoon vegetable oil
    ½ cup chopped parsley
    1 teaspoon basil
    2 cups milk
    1 cup light (table) cream
    Salt and pepper to taste
    ¼ cup toasted sliced almonds for garnish
    2 tablespoons sherry (optional)

Prepare squash by peeling, seeding, and cutting into chunks. Place in large saucepan with water and salt; simmer until done.

Meanwhile sauté onion in oil until tender.

Place squash, cooking water, and onion in blender; liquefy. Add parsley, basil, milk, and cream; blend. (Blend in 2 lots if necessary.) Add salt, pepper, and sherry; heat.

Serve soup with almonds sprinkled on top as garnish.

beef vegetable soup

Yield: 6 main-course servings

1½ pounds boneless round steak,
    cut into ½-inch cubes
3 tablespoons vegetable oil
1 medium onion, chopped
2 carrots, chopped
½ green pepper, chopped
2 stalks celery, chopped

1½ cups chopped cabbage
2 tablespoons tomato paste
1 teaspoon salt
½ teaspoon pepper
1 parsley stalk
1 bay leaf
½ teaspoon thyme

Brown meat in hot oil in Dutch oven. Remove; reserve.

Add vegetables (except tomato paste) to Dutch oven; stir-cook until wilted. Return meat to Dutch oven. Add remaining ingredients. Pour in enough boiling water to cover ingredients. Cover; simmer gently about 2 hours or until meat is tender. Remove bay leaf and parsley.

Serve soup with French bread for a light and nutritious dinner.

beef vegetable soup

chicken corn chowder

Yield: 3 quarts

> 3 medium onions, chopped
> 1 clove garlic, minced
> ¼ cup butter or margarine
> 1 stalk celery, including leaves, chopped
> 1 quart chicken stock or bouillon
> 2 medium potatoes, peeled, diced
> 1 bay leaf
> 1 teaspoon salt
> ⅔ cup dry milk powder
> 1 10-ounce package frozen corn (or 2 cups fresh)
> 1 16-ounce can kidney beans, drained (or 1½ cups cooked kidney beans)
> 1 cup diced cooked chicken
> Dash of freshly ground black pepper

Fry onions and garlic in butter in Dutch oven over medium heat until onions are transparent and tender. Add celery; cook until celery is tender, stirring occasionally. Stir in broth, potatoes, bay leaf, and salt. Cover; simmer until potatoes are tender, about 30 minutes. Remove from heat; puree in blender. Blend small amounts at a time. Put back into Dutch oven; let cool slightly. Stir in milk powder, corn, beans, chicken, and pepper. Heat again, just until corn is tender; be careful not to overcook corn. Ladle into bowls.

chicken 'n cheese vegetable chowder

Yield: 4 to 6 servings

> 3 cups chicken broth
> 1½ cups sliced carrots
> 1 10-ounce package frozen chopped broccoli
> 1 tablespoon dehydrated minced onion
> ¾ teaspoon salt
> ⅛ teaspoon pepper
> ⅛ teaspoon ground marjoram
> ¼ cup whole-wheat flour
> 1 cup nonfat dry milk powder
> 1½ cups water
> 1½ cups chopped cooked chicken
> 1 cup grated cheddar cheese

Combine broth, carrots, broccoli, onion, salt, pepper, and marjoram in large saucepan or Dutch oven. Bring to boil; reduce heat. Cover; simmer until carrots are tender, about 10 minutes.

Stir together flour and milk powder. Beat in water until dry ingredients are smooth. Stir into hot mixture. Simmer, stirring occasionally, about 10 minutes. Do not let mixture boil.

Turn heat off. Stir in chicken and cheese. Cover; let stand until cheese melts.

vichyssoise

Yield: 4 servings

3 to 4 leeks or green onions
2 tablespoons butter or margarine
1 medium onion, chopped
2 large potatoes, peeled, diced
½ teaspoon salt
3 cups chicken broth

1½ cups milk
1 cup heavy cream
1 drop Tabasco sauce
1 tablespoon minced parsley or chives

Thoroughly clean leeks. Halve lengthwise; cut into thin slices.

Heat butter. Add leeks and onion; cook until transparent. Add potatoes, salt, and broth; simmer 35 minutes. Puree in blender or food mill; reheat. Pour in milk and ½ cup cream. Heat and stir until well blended, but do not boil. Season with Tabasco sauce. Chill mixture.

Beat ½ cup cream until stiff; fold into soup. Adjust seasonings.

Serve soup garnished with chopped chives or parsley.

broccoli chowder

Yield: 4 servings

1 pound fresh broccoli
1½ cups chicken broth
1½ cups milk
½ cup chopped cooked ham
¼ teaspoon freshly ground pepper
1½ cups grated Swiss cheese (6 ounces)
2 tablespoons butter or margarine
Salt to taste

broccoli chowder

Wash broccoli; remove leaves and coarse stem ends.

Pour broth into large pot; bring to boil. Add broccoli. Reduce heat; simmer, uncovered, 3 minutes. Cover; cook 10 minutes or until broccoli is just tender. Remove broccoli with slotted spoon; chop into bite-size pieces.

Add milk, ham, and pepper to stock. Bring to boil, stirring occasionally. Stir in cheese, butter, and broccoli; heat until cheese is melted. Add salt to taste. Do not boil. Serve hot.

Picture on opposite page: vichyssoise

clam chowder

Yield: 4 to 6 servings

>1 small onion, minced
>2 tablespoons butter or margarine
>1 10½-ounce can minced clams
>1 cup boiling water (clam broth may be substituted for part of water)
>1 large potato, diced
>½ teaspoon salt
>⅛ teaspoon pepper
>1 tablespoon flour
>1 tablespoon cold water
>1 cup evaporated milk
>1 cup water

Sauté onion in butter until golden brown. Add clams; simmer 5 minutes. Add boiling water, potato, salt, and pepper. Simmer, covered, 30 minutes.

Mix flour with cold water. Add to clam mixture; stir and heat until thickened. Add milk and 1 cup water to chowder; heat through.

Serve with chowder crackers.

stuffed flank steak

Yield: 4 to 6 servings

2 pounds flank steak, scored, or 2 round steaks, thinly sliced
2 tablespoons Dijon-style mustard
¼ teaspoon thyme

Spread meat with mustard; sprinkle with thyme.

spinach stuffing

½ package frozen spinach, cooked, drained
½ cup chopped onions
1 tablespoon bacon fat or vegetable oil
½ cup raw sausage meat
1 egg
½ teaspoon salt
⅛ teaspoon allspice
⅛ teaspoon pepper
1 clove garlic, crushed
¼ cup dry bread crumbs

Squeeze all water from spinach.
Sauté onions in fat. Add spinach; toss. Add sausage, egg, salt, allspice, pepper, garlic, and crumbs to spinach mixture; mix well. Spread stuffing on meat; roll up jelly-roll fashion. Tie with string.

6 slices bacon
1 onion, chopped
1 carrot, chopped
½ cup dry white wine
1 can beef broth

Cook bacon in Dutch oven until partly done; remove.
Add meat to Dutch oven; brown on all sides (about 10 minutes). Lay bacon over meat. Add onion, carrot, wine, and broth; bring to simmer. Place in 325°F oven about 1 hour or until tender.
Place meat on platter. Strain juices, pressing hard on vegetables. If desired, thicken with 1 tablespoon cornstarch dissolved in water.
Slice meat; serve with pan juices.

beef braised in red wine

Yield: 6 servings

3 to 4 pounds boneless beef roast (rump, sirloin tip, or round)
½ teaspoon salt
¼ teaspoon freshly ground black pepper

marinade

3 cups red wine
1 cup water
½ cup sliced onions
¼ cup sliced carrots

1 clove garlic, minced
1 bay leaf, crumbled
2 teaspoons chopped fresh parsley
1 teaspoon thyme

braising ingredients

2 tablespoons vegetable oil
2 strips lean bacon, cubed
1 ounce brandy, warmed
1 veal or beef knuckle
1 tomato, peeled, quartered

1 tablespoon chopped fresh parsley
1 bay leaf
3 green onions, chopped
1 cup beef bouillon
½ teaspoon salt

vegetables

10 small white onions, peeled
8 carrots, peeled, shaped like small balls
Parsley for garnish

2 tablespoons flour
2 tablespoons butter or margarine
3 tablespoons Madeira

Rub beef with salt; sprinkle with pepper.

Blend all marinade ingredients. Pour into glass or ceramic bowl. Add beef; turn several times, so that all sides are coated with marinade. Cover; marinate in refrigerator 12 to 24 hours. Turn roast occasionally.

Remove roast from marinade; drain. Pat dry with paper towels. Strain and reserve marinade.

Heat oil in large Dutch oven. Add bacon; cook until transparent. Add roast; brown well on all sides. Drain off fat. Pour brandy over meat. Ignite; let flames die down. Add remaining braising ingredients; cover pan. Place in preheated 350°F oven. During cooking, occasionally pour some marinade over roast. Cook 3 hours.

Meanwhile, prepare vegetables. Add onions and carrots to Dutch oven; braise 1 hour.

When meat and vegetables are tender, remove meat from oven; place on pre-heated platter. Surround with onions and carrots. Garnish with parsley. Keep food warm.

Strain sauce through fine sieve. Skim off fat if necessary.

Cream together flour and butter; thicken pan sauce with all or part. Stir and heat to boiling 1 to 2 minutes. Add Madeira; adjust seasonings. Spoon some sauce over meat; serve rest separately.

beef braised in red wine

soybean beef bake

This casserole is especially good if made early in the day and baked later!

Yield: 5 to 6 servings

½ pound lean ground beef
1 medium onion, chopped
2 stalks celery (including leaves), chopped
1 8-ounce can (1 cup) tomato sauce
⅔ cup water
2 tablespoons soy sauce
¾ teaspoon salt
½ teaspoon oregano
Dash of pepper
2 cups cooked soybeans
2 cups cooked rice
¼ cup Parmesan cheese
2 tablespoons toasted wheat germ

Sauté beef and onion together in frypan. Add celery; cook until meat has browned. Lower heat to simmer. Stir in tomato sauce, water, soy sauce, salt, oregano, and pepper. Add soybeans and rice. Pour into greased 2-quart casserole. Top with mixture of cheese and wheat germ. Bake in 350°F oven 30 minutes.

scandinavian pot roast

Yield: 6 servings

¼ cup vegetable oil
1 3-pound rump or round roast
¼ pound small fresh mushrooms
3 medium onions, thinly sliced
1 clove garlic
½ teaspoon salt
¼ teaspoon pepper

¼ teaspoon ginger
½ cup red wine
2 cups beef broth
12 pitted prunes
¼ cup black olives, drained
Parsley for garnish

Heat oil in large Dutch oven; brown meat on all sides. Remove meat; reserve. Sauté mushrooms in same oil. Remove; reserve.

Add onions and garlic to oil; cook until onions are soft and golden. Drain off remaining oil. Return meat to Dutch oven. Add seasonings, wine, and broth. Cook, covered, in 300°F oven 2 hours. Add prunes and olives; cook 1 hour or until roast is tender. Add mushrooms; heat through.

Place roast on platter; surround with mushrooms, prunes, and olives. If desired, reduce stock by boiling. Pour over meat, or serve separately. Sprinkle top of roast and sauce with finely chopped parsley.

scandinavian pot roast

beef goulash

beef goulash

Yield: 4 servings

    1 pound lean beef (round steak)
2 tablespoons vegetable oil
1 large onion, chopped
1 pound potatoes, peeled, cubed
1 green pepper, cut into strips
2 tomatoes, peeled, cut into chunks
1 clove garlic, minced
½ teaspoon caraway seeds
1 3-inch piece lemon peel, minced
2 teaspoons paprika
½ teaspoon salt
2 cups beef bouillon

Pat meat dry with paper towels. Cut into strips approximately ½ inch wide and 2 inches long.

Heat oil in 4-quart Dutch oven. Add meat and onion; cook 5 minutes or until brown. Add potatoes; cook 5 minutes. Add remaining ingredients. Cover; simmer over low heat 30 minutes. At end of cooking time, uncover; boil liquid a few minutes, until reduced. Correct seasoning if necessary.

31

stuffed eggplant

Yield: 4 to 6 servings

1 large eggplant
½ cup chopped onion
1 cup chopped mushrooms
1 pound lean ground beef
2 tablespoons vegetable oil
2 tablespoons tomato paste
¼ cup wheat germ
1 teaspoon basil
½ teaspoon chervil
½ teaspoon salt
¼ teaspoon pepper
Parsley for garnish

Cut eggplant in half lengthwise. Remove pulp, leaving ½ inch of shell; chop pulp.

Sauté onion, mushrooms, and meat in hot oil. Add tomato paste, wheat germ, seasonings, and eggplant pulp. Cook until meat is almost done. Spoon meat mixture into eggplant shell; set in greased ovenproof dish. Bake in preheated 350°F oven 30 minutes.

Garnish eggplant with parsley.

hamburger–cheese quiche

Yield: 6 servings

1 pound ground beef
1 medium onion, chopped
1 teaspoon salt
¼ teaspoon pepper
1 partially baked quiche or Pie Crust (see Index)
½ cup sliced mushrooms
2 eggs, beaten
6 ounces cheddar cheese, grated
¼ teaspoon paprika

Sauté beef and onion until onion is tender. Stir in salt and pepper. Spread beef on pie crust. Top with layer of mushrooms.

Mix eggs with cheese; spread on top of mushrooms. Sprinkle with paprika. Bake at 350°F 20 to 30 minutes.

hidden-layer meat loaf

Yield: 6 servings

filling

1 medium onion, chopped
2 tablespoons butter or margarine
2 cups sliced mushrooms
1 tablespoon parsley flakes
¼ teaspoon salt

Dash of pepper
1 tablespoon all-purpose flour
½ cup yogurt
1 tablespoon grated Parmesan cheese

Sauté onion in butter until soft. Add mushrooms, parsley, salt, and pepper. Sauté just until mushrooms become juicy. Stir in flour, yogurt, and cheese. Set aside.

meat mixture

½ cup bread crumbs
1½ pounds lean ground beef
½ cup water
1 egg
¼ cup nonfat dry milk powder

1 stalk celery, cut into chunks
¾ teaspoon salt
⅛ teaspoon pepper
½ teaspoon Worcestershire sauce

Add bread crumbs to beef.

Place remaining ingredients in blender; blend smooth. Add to meat; stir until evenly combined.

Grease 10-inch bundt baking pan. Place half of meat mixture in pan. Press center of meat ring to make slight indentation. Pour filling over. Top with remaining meat mixture. Bake at 350°F 1 hour. Let stand 5 minutes; remove from pan.

To serve, garnish with fresh parsley; fill center with mashed potatoes or other vegetables if desired.

witch casserole

Yield: 4 servings

2 slices bacon
½ cup sliced onion
½ pound ground beef
1 teaspoon salt
2 cups cooked lentils (cooked according to package directions)
1 cup canned tomatoes with juice
4 tablespoons Parmesan cheese

Fry bacon in large frypan until crisp; remove and reserve bacon.
Sauté onion in bacon fat until transparent. Remove onion; reserve.
Brown beef in fat. Drain excess fat from beef.
Crumble bacon. Combine bacon, onion, meat, salt, and lentils. Place in lightly greased casserole. Top with tomatoes; cover with layer of cheese. Bake, covered, 30 minutes at 350°F.

susan's spaghetti with meat sauce

Yield: 1½ quarts sauce, or 8 servings

meat sauce

1 pound lean ground beef
1 small onion, finely chopped
½ green pepper, finely chopped
1 15-ounce can tomato sauce
1 12-ounce can tomato paste
1 4½-ounce can chopped ripe olives, drained
1 4-ounce can mushroom pieces, drained, chopped
1½ cups water
1 teaspoon sugar
1½ teaspoons salt
1 teaspoon pepper
1 teaspoon oregano
1 teaspoon thyme
½ teaspoon basil
1 clove galric, crushed
1 bay leaf

Combine meat and onion in Dutch oven; cook until meat is browned and onion is tender. Skim off excess fat. Add remaining ingredients. Cover; simmer 1½ hours. Partially cover; simmer 1 hour or until sauce is thick. Stir occasionally during cooking.

8 ounces spaghetti
2 teaspoons butter or margarine
⅓ cup Parmesan cheese
1 tablespoon chopped fresh parsley

Cook spaghetti according to package directions; drain. Stir in butter and half the cheese.

Remove bay leaf from sauce; spoon sauce over spaghetti. Sprinkle with remaining cheese and parsley.

easy family "tacos"

Children especially enjoy this version of tacos because it is easy to handle when eaten with a fork or spoon, and everyone can add or subtract toppings according to his own taste.

Yield: 6 servings

1½ pounds lean ground beef
1 medium onion, chopped
1 clove garlic, minced
1 teaspoon salt
½ teaspoon oregano
Pinch of cumin powder
1 teaspoon chili powder
½ 15-ounce can (2 cups) tomato sauce
2 tablespoons catsup
1 12-ounce bag natural corn chips, partially crushed
2 cups shredded Monterey Jack cheese
Several fresh tomatoes, diced
Chopped lettuce
Chopped ripe olives

Sauté meat and onion in large frying pan until meat has browned and onion is tender. Stir in garlic, salt, oregano, cumin, and chili powder. Add tomato sauce. Stir in catsup; simmer over low heat, uncovered, 10 to 15 minutes. While meat mixture is simmering, make Taco Sauce.

taco sauce

½ 15-ounce can tomato sauce
1 tablespoon cider vinegar
1 clove garlic, crushed
2 teaspoons vegetable oil
1 4-ounce can chopped green chilies, drained
Few drops hot pepper sauce, to taste

Heat all ingredients together in small saucepan. Simmer over low heat about 10 minutes, or until ready to serve tacos.

To serve, place meat sauce and corn chips in separate serving bowls. Arrange small dishes of cheese, lettuce, olives, tomatoes, and Taco Sauce nearby. Spoon meat sauce over corn chips on each plate, then help yourself to toppings, starting with cheese, tomatoes, olives, lettuce, and Taco Sauce.

corned beef–stuffed potatoes

Yield: 4 servings

4 large baking potatoes
1½ cups minced cooked corned beef
¼ cup butter or margarine
Salt and pepper to taste
⅛ cup minced fresh parsley
4 eggs

Bake potatoes at 400°F 1 hour or until done. Cut slice off top of each potato; scoop out centers. Leave ¼ to ½ inch potato around walls. Mash potatoes. Stir in corned beef and butter. Add salt and pepper. Divide mixture among potatoes; reheat.

Meanwhile poach eggs.

Sprinkle tops of potatoes with parsley; top with cooked eggs. Serve as a main dish.

corned-beef stuffed potatoes

braised veal rolls

braised veal rolls

Yield: 4 servings

 4 veal scallops or cutlets
 1 onion, chopped
 4 tablespoons vegetable oil
 4 ounces mushrooms, minced
     (about 1 cup)
 1 clove garlic, minced
 2 large carrots, chopped
 1 large onion, chopped
 ¾ cup white wine
 ¾ cup beef broth
 ½ teaspoon salt
 ⅛ teaspoon pepper
 ¼ teaspoon thyme
 1 bay leaf
 1 tablespoon butter or margarine
 1 tablespoon flour
 Parlsey for garnish

Pound veal to tenderize and flatten.

In large frypan sauté 1 onion in 2 tablespoons hot oil until soft. Add mushrooms; cook 5 minutes. Spread onion–mushroom mixture on each slice of meat. Roll up; tie with string.

Brown veal in 2 tablespoons hot oil. Remove; reserve. Drain excess oil.

Add garlic, carrots, large onion, wine, broth, salt, pepper, thyme, and bay leaf to frypan. Heat to simmer. Add veal; cover. Simmer 1½ hours.

When veal is done, remove strings from rolls. Place on serving dish; keep warm.

Remove bay leaf from sauce. Pour sauce into electric blender; puree.

If thicker sauce is desired, melt butter in saucepan. Stir in flour; make smooth paste. Add sauce, stirring constantly; heat to boiling point. Reduce heat to simmer; cook 1 to 2 minutes, until sauce thickens.

Pour sauce over veal rolls; garnish with chopped parsley. Serve with boiled potatoes if desired.

country casserole

Yield: 6 servings

1 pound Great Northern beans
6 cups water
2 medium onions, chopped
½ teaspoon salt
¼ teaspoon pepper
1 bay leaf
3 whole cloves
2 tablespoons butter or margarine
1 tablespoon vegetable oil
1 pound boned lamb (shoulder or leg), cut into 2-inch chunks
½ pound pork, cut into 1½-inch chunks
1 stalk celery, thinly sliced
1 carrot, thinly sliced
2 green onions, chopped
½ pound Polish sausage, thinly sliced
1 cup red wine
2 tablespoons tomato paste
2 cloves garlic, minced
3 tablespoons chopped parsley
Dash of cayenne pepper
1 to 2 cups beef bouillon
2 tablespoons packaged bread crumbs

Wash beans. Place in pan with 6 cups water. Bring to boil; boil 2 minutes. Remove from heat; let stand, covered, 1 hour.

Add 2 onions, salt, pepper, bay leaf, and cloves to beans in their soaking liquid. Cover; cook 1 hour. When done, drain beans; reserve liquid.

Meanwhile heat 1 tablespoon butter and oil in frypan; fry lamb and pork until brown. Add celery, carrot, green onions, and sausage. Pour in wine; simmer 40 minutes. Stir in tomato paste, garlic, and parsley; season with cayenne. Simmer 5 minutes, stirring occasionally. Add beans; mix thoroughly.

Grease ovenproof casserole; spoon in mixture. Add enough bean liquid or bouillon to come to top of bean–meat mixture. Sprinkle with bread crumbs; dot with 1 tablespoon butter. Bake in preheated 375°F oven 1 hour.

Serve casserole with chunks of French bread and red wine.

Picture on opposite page: country casserole

vegetable stew with lamb

Yield: 6 servings

2 tablespoons vegetable oil
1 pound lean lamb, cut into bite-size pieces
1 medium onion, chopped
1 small head cabbage, shredded
1 stalk celery, sliced
2 medium carrots, sliced
1 stalk leek, sliced
6 cups hot beef bouillon
2 medium potatoes, cubed
1 small head cauliflower, separated into florets
1 10-ounce package frozen green beans
2 tablespoons tomato paste
½ teaspoon salt
¼ teaspoon white pepper
Parsley to garnish

Heat oil in 4-quart Dutch oven or saucepan. Brown meat about 5 minutes. Add onion; sauté until golden brown. Add cabbage, celery, carrots, leek, and bouillon. Bring to boil; simmer 1 hour. Add potatoes, cauliflower, and beans. Simmer 20 to 30 minutes, until vegetables are tender.

Thin tomato paste with a little broth; add to stew. Season with salt and pepper. Garnish stew with chopped parsley.

vegetable stew with lamb

irish stew

Yield: 6 servings

1½ pounds boneless lamb, cut into
    1-inch cubes
1 tablespoon vegetable oil
2 cups boiling water
1 cup cubed turnips or rutabagas
1 cup sliced carrots
1 cup cubed potatoes

½ cup chopped onions
2 teaspoons salt
½ teaspoon paprika
1 teaspoon celery seed
1 cup peas, fresh or frozen
1 tablespoon flour
¼ cup cold water

In Dutch oven brown meat in hot oil. Add boiling water; cover. Simmer 1 hour. Add vegetables (except peas) and seasonings; cover. Cook 40 minutes or until vegetables are done and meat tender.

Meanwhile cook peas in small amount boiling water until done. Drain; reserve.

In small dish mix flour with cold water; stir well to break up lumps.

When stew is done, thicken broth with flour–water combination. Simmer to allow starch to cook. Add cooked peas; heat through.

shish kabob on rice

Yield: 4 servings

⅓ cup vegetable oil
⅓ cup soy sauce
1 onion, sliced
¼ teaspoon oregano
¼ teaspoon basil
½ teaspoon rosemary
¼ teaspoon thyme
2 pounds lean boned lamb
    (leg or shoulder)

¼ cup butter or margarine
1 cup brown rice
2 tablespoons minced onion
3 cups chicken broth
2 green peppers
2 firm tomatoes, quartered
8 medium mushrooms

Mix together oil, soy sauce, sliced onion, and seasonings.

Cube meat into 1½-inch chunks; place in glass or ceramic casserole. Add marinade; cover. Refrigerate 24 hours, turning meat at least twice.

About 1¼ hours before dinner is to be served, melt butter in saucepan. Add rice and minced onion; cook, stirring constantly, until onion is golden brown. Add broth; cover. Simmer 1 hour or until all water is absorbed and rice is tender.

Meanwhile cut peppers into 1½-inch squares. Alternate lamb, green pepper, tomatoes, and mushrooms on 4 large skewers. Brush with marinade. Place on broiler rack; start broiling just before rice is done. Broil about 4 inches from flame 6 to 8 minutes on each side.

Spoon rice into serving dish; place kabobs on rice.

pork with red-cabbage casserole

Yield: 6 servings

4 strips bacon, diced
1 quart water
1 carrot, thinly sliced
1 large onion, sliced
2 tablespoons butter or margarine
2 pounds red cabbage, cut into ½-inch strips
2 tart apples, diced
1 clove garlic, mashed
1 bay leaf

⅛ teaspoon clove
⅛ teaspoon nutmeg
½ teaspoon salt
¼ teaspoon pepper
2 cups red wine
2 cups beef bouillon
3 pounds boneless pork roast
2 tablespoons vegetable oil

Simmer bacon in water about 10 minutes; drain. Cook bacon, carrot, and onion in butter in covered ovenproof casserole over low heat 10 minutes. Do not brown. Stir in cabbage; mix well. Cover; cook slowly 15 minutes. Stir in all remaining ingredients except meat and vegetable oil. Simmer 2 to 3 minutes on top of range. Cover; place in preheated 325°F oven. Simmer slowly about 3 hours.

Just before cabbage is finished cooking, brown pork in hot oil. Place in casserole with cabbage; cover. Simmer 2 hours or until pork is done. Correct seasonings.

pork with cider sauce

Yield: 4 servings

1½ pounds lean boneless pork, cut into 1-inch cubes
⅓ cup flour
⅓ cup vegetable oil
1½ cups apple cider or apple juice
2 carrots, sliced
1 small onion, sliced
½ teaspoon rosemary
1 bay leaf
1 teaspoon salt
½ teaspoon pepper

Thoroughly dredge pork with flour.

Heat oil in large frypan until hot. Carefully add pork; cook until browned on all sides. Remove pork; drain on paper towels. Place in casserole.

Drain oil from pan. Pour cider into pan; heat and stir to remove browned pieces from pan.

Add carrots, onion, rosemary, bay leaf, salt, pepper, and hot cider to casserole; cover. Bake in 325°F oven 2 hours or until meat is tender. Remove bay leaf.

pork with cider sauce

party pork chops

fresh vegetables with pork

Yield: 8 servings

> 8 thick-sliced (¾-inch) pork chops
> 8 onion slices, about ¼ inch thick
> 8 fresh lemon slices, about ¼ inch thick, from midsections of 2 unpeeled lemons
> ⅔ cup brown sugar
> 1¼ teaspoons salt
> ¼ teaspoon pepper
> 3 tablespoons fresh lemon juice
> ⅔ cup chili sauce

Place pork in single layer in baking pan. Place 1 onion slice topped with 1 lemon slice on center of each chop.

Blend remaining ingredients; spoon over each chop. Cover pan tightly. Bake in 350°F oven 1½ hours or until pork is tender.

fresh vegetables with pork

Yield: 6 servings

> 2 tablespoons vegetable oil
> 6 stalks celery, sliced diagonally
> ½ pound mushrooms, halved
> 1 medium green pepper, sliced
> 1 medium red pepper, sliced
> 1 medium onion, sliced
> 1 pound boneless pork, cut into ½-inch cubes
> 1 cup chicken broth
> 1 tablespoon soy sauce
> 1 tablespoon cornstarch
> ½ teaspoon ginger
> ¼ teaspoon pepper

Heat oil in wok or frypan. Stir-fry celery about 4 minutes. Add mushrooms, peppers, and onion; stir-fry 5 minutes. Remove vegetables; reserve.

Add pork to pan; stir-fry 5 minutes. Add broth; stir in vegetables. Simmer 5 minutes.

Meanwhile blend soy sauce with cornstarch, ginger, and pepper. Stir into pork and vegetable mixture; cook, stirring constantly, about 3 minutes or until heated and thickened.

Serve mixture over rice.

sausage pizza

Yield: 12-inch pizza

sausage pizza

pizza crust

> 1 package active dry
>   yeast
> ½ cup warm water
>   (105 to 115°F)
> ¾ cup all-purpose flour
>   and ¾ cup whole wheat flour
>   (or 1½ cups all-purpose flour
>   if desired)
> ½ teaspoon salt
> 1 teaspoon sugar
> 1 tablespoon vegetable oil

pizza sauce

> ¼ cup chopped onion
> 1 tablespoon vegetable oil
> 1 16-ounce can tomatoes
> 3 tablespoons tomato paste
> 1 teaspoon oregano
> ½ teaspoon salt
> ⅛ teaspoon freshly ground black pepper

pizza toppings*

> 1 tablespoon vegetable oil
> ¼ to ½ pound bulk sausage
> 6 ounces mozzarella cheese, shredded
> 2 tablespoons Parmesan cheese

> *Other toppings, such as mushrooms, ham, anchovy fillets, pepperoni, etc.,
>   can be added if desired.

In medium bowl dissolve yeast in warm water.

Combine flours, salt, and sugar in separate bowl. Add flour mixture and oil to yeast; stir well. Turn out onto floured board; knead until smooth and elastic, about 6 to 8 minutes.

Lightly grease bowl. Place dough in bowl; turn once to grease top surface. Cover; let rise until double in bulk (about 1½ hours).

Meanwhile in medium frypan sauté onion in hot oil until tender. Add remaining sauce ingredients. Break up tomato pieces with fork. Bring sauce to boil; reduce heat to low. Cook, partially covered, 50 minutes or until thick; cool.

When dough has doubled in bulk, punch down. Roll out into 12-inch circle; place on round pizza pan or cookie sheet. Brush lightly with oil. Let rise 10 minutes. Bake crust 10 minutes in preheated 400°F oven.

While crust is cooking, lightly fry sausage. Remove the crust from oven; top with sauce. Then top with sausage; sprinkle cheeses over all. Bake 12 minutes or until cheese is melted and lightly browned. Remove pizza from pan; cut and enjoy.

savory sausage quiche

Yield: 4 to 6 servings

> 1 pound bulk sausage
> 1 cup fresh mushrooms, sliced
> 1 large onion, thinly sliced
> ⅓ cup chopped celery
> 1⅓ cups grated cheddar cheese
> 1 cup milk
> 3 eggs, beaten
> 2 tablespoons all-purpose flour
> ½ teaspoon salt
> 1 10-inch Whole-Wheat Pie Crust (see Index), baked 6 to 8 minutes, then cooled
> ¼ teaspoon paprika
> Dash of nutmeg

Brown sausage in frying pan until partially cooked. Remove from pan; let drain on paper towels.

Pour all but 1 tablespoon fat out of pan. Sauté mushrooms, onion, and celery until tender but not brown.

Place sausage and vegetables in pie crust. Add 1 cup cheese.

Beat together milk, eggs, flour, and salt. Pour into pie shell. Spread remaining cheese over top of mixture. Sprinkle paprika and nutmeg over all. Bake in 400°F oven 30 minutes.

sausage-stuffed acorn squash

Yield: 4 servings

> 2 acorn squash
> 1 pound bulk sausage
> 3 tablespoons chopped onion
> 1 teaspoon salt
> 2 apples, cored, chopped
> ½ teaspoon oregano

Cut squash in half crosswise; scoop out seeds. Place squash cut-side-down in baking pan containing 1 inch hot water. Bake at 375°F 45 minutes or until squash is soft.

Meanwhile sauté sausage in frypan. Break meat into chunks with fork. Remove sausage; set aside.

Drain fat, except 2 tablespoons. Add onion; sauté until tender. Return sausage with remaining ingredients to frypan; toss lightly to combine.

Fill squash halves with sausage mixture. Return squash, filling-side-up, to baking dish. Replenish water if necessary. Bake, uncovered, 20 minutes.

ham and cheese grits

Yield: 6 servings

    4 cups water
    1 teaspoon salt
    1 cup quick grits
    2 eggs, beaten
    ¼ cup nonfat dry milk powder
    ¼ cup butter or margarine
    2 cups shredded cheddar cheese
    1 cup cubed cooked ham
    1 garlic clove, minced (optional)
    1 tablespoon parsley flakes

Bring water and salt to boiling in saucepan. Slowly stir in grits. Cook over low heat, stirring occasionally, about 5 minutes. Remove from heat.

Beat together eggs and dry milk. Add small amount hot grits to egg mixture while stirring. Slowly add eggs to hot grits, stirring constantly. Blend in butter, cheese, ham, and garlic. Pour into greased 2-quart casserole. Sprinkle with parsley. Bake at 350°F 45 to 50 minutes or until set.

vermont breakfast pie

Yield: 4 to 6 servings

    2 medium apples, peeled, cored, sliced
    3 tablespoons butter or margarine
    ¼ teaspoon cinnamon
    Dash of nutmeg
    2 eggs, beaten
    ¼ cup all-purpose flour
    ¼ cup whole-wheat pastry flour
    ¼ teaspoon salt
    ½ cup milk
    2 slices (2 ounces) boiled ham
    ½ cup grated cheddar cheese

Sauté apples in butter until soft. Stir in cinnamon and nutmeg.

Beat together eggs, flours, salt, and milk with egg beater or electric mixer. (Do *not* use blender.) Fold in apple mixture. Pour into 9-inch pie pan or shallow baking dish. Bake in preheated 425°F oven 20 minutes.

While mixture is baking, cut ham diagonally into quarters.

Remove pie from oven when done; arrange ham triangles on top. Sprinkle with cheese. Return to oven until cheese is just melted. Serve pie hot.

ham and fruit in pineapple

Yield: 2 servings

1 fresh pineapple

ham stuffing

6 ounces cooked ham, cubed
6 ounces sauerkraut
1 medium apple

salad dressing

3 tablespoons mayonnaise
2 tablespoons light (table) cream
Juice of 1 lemon
1 teaspoon fresh chopped dill or ¼ teaspoon dried dill
¼ teaspoon rosemary
¼ teaspoon sugar
Salt if desired

Cut pineapple into half lengthwise; scoop out. Cut into bite-size pieces.
Cube ham.
Rinse and drain sauerkraut.
Core unpeeled apple; cut into thin slices.
Gently mix above ingredients. Fill pineapple halves with Ham Stuffing.
Thoroughly blend mayonnaise, cream, lemon juice, dill, rosemary, sugar, and
salt. Pour dressing over salad. Let marinate and chill in refrigerator 30 minutes.

poultry

chicken lentil casserole

Yield: 4 to 5 servings

1 cup lentils
2½ cups water
3 tablespoons butter or margarine
½ pound mushrooms, sliced
1 medium onion, chopped
1 large carrot, chopped
1 medium potato, chopped
1 tablespoon all-purpose flour
1½ cups seasoned chicken broth
¾ teaspoon salt
⅛ teaspoon pepper
¾ teaspoon dillweed
1 cup chopped cooked chicken
1 cup buttered whole-wheat bread crumbs

Wash lentils. Place in saucepan; cover with water. Bring to boil; cover. Simmer over low heat 20 minutes.

Melt 2 tablespoons butter in frying pan. Sauté mushrooms lightly. Remove mushrooms; set aside.

Add remaining butter to pan. Sauté onion, carrot, and potato until onion is soft. Stir in flour; mix thoroughly. Add broth, salt, pepper, and dillweed; boil, stirring, about 1 minute. Remove from heat. Add mushrooms and chicken.

Drain lentils. Stir into sauce. Pour into 1½-quart casserole dish. Top with buttered bread crumbs. Bake at 350°F about 30 minutes, until lightly browned and bubbly.

spicy roast chicken

Yield: 4 servings

> 1 cup plain yogurt
> 3 cloves garlic, crushed
> 2 teaspoons grated fresh ginger
> ⅓ cup lime juice
> 1 tablespoon ground coriander
> 1 teaspoon cumin
> ½ teaspoon cayenne pepper
> 1 whole chicken (3 pounds)
> Lime wedges
> 1 onion, sliced, steamed

Mix yogurt, garlic, ginger, lime juice, and spices. Rub chicken inside and out with mixture. Place in bowl; pour remaining marinade over. Cover; refrigerate 24 hours. Turn chicken at least once.

Remove chicken from marinade. Roast in preheated 375°F oven 1 hour or until done. Baste with marinade during cooking.

Disjoint chicken; serve with lime wedges and onion slices.

judy's chicken curry

Yield: 4 to 6 servings

> 1 frying chicken, cut into serving pieces
> 2 tablespoons vegetable oil
> 2 tablespoons butter or margarine
> 2 cups cooked barley
> 1 medium onion, minced
> 2 cups chicken broth
> Salt and pepper to taste
> 2 teaspoons curry powder
> 1 teaspoon marjoram
> 1 cup plain yogurt
> 1 tomato, peeled, seeded, cut into bite-size pieces

Brown chicken in oil and butter in large skillet. Remove chicken from pan; place on bed of barley in Dutch oven or flameproof casserole dish.

Cook onion until transparent in same skillet in remaining oil and butter. Remove; place on top of chicken.

Pour 1½ cups broth over chicken and barley. Sprinkle with salt, pepper, curry powder, and marjoram. Cover; cook over low heat 30 minutes.

Remove cover. Add yogurt, tomato, and ½ cup broth if needed. Cook, uncovered, 20 to 30 minutes, until chicken is tender.

chicken paprika

Yield: 4 servings

1 chicken, 2½ to 3 pounds
1 tablespoon vegetable oil
1 large onion, chopped
2 tablespoons paprika
1 clove garlic, minced
½ teaspoon salt
1 teaspoon caraway seeds
1 cup hot water
1 scallion or leek, cut lengthwise, sliced

1 small carrot, sliced
1 small stalk celery, sliced
2 medium potatoes, peeled, cubed
½ cup chicken broth or bouillon
3 tomatoes
1 red pepper, cubed
1 green pepper, cubed
Parsley for garnish

Skin and bone chicken; cut into bite-size pieces.

Heat oil in 4-quart Dutch oven; sauté onion. Sprinkle 1 tablespoon paprika over onion; stir well. Add garlic, salt, caraway seeds, and ½ cup hot water. Simmer over low heat 10 minutes. Add chicken pieces; cover. Simmer 5 minutes. Add ½ cup water; cover. Simmer 15 minutes. Add scallion, carrot, celery, potatoes, and broth. Simmer 10 minutes.

Peel and chop 2 tomatoes.

Add peppers, chopped tomatoes, and 1 tablespoon paprika to chicken; cover. Simmer 15 minutes. Correct seasoning if necessary.

Serve chicken garnished with 1 sliced tomato and chopped parsley.

chicken paprika

51

pineapple chicken with poppy-seed noodles

Yield: 4 servings

4 chicken breasts
Salt and pepper to taste
2 tablespoons butter or margarine

8 ounces spinach noodles
1 chicken bouillon cube (optional)
2 tablespoons poppy seeds

Sprinkle chicken with salt and pepper; sauté in 1 tablespoon butter in large frying pan until browned. Cover; cook over low heat until tender, about 25 to 30 minutes.

While chicken is cooking, cook noodles in boiling salted water seasoned with bouillon cube just until tender, about 8 to 10 minutes. Drain; season with 1 tablespoon butter and poppy seeds. Place in large shallow ovenproof dish. When chicken has finished cooking, place on top of noodles; cover. Keep warm while preparing dressing and sauce.

dressing

1 small onion, chopped
½ pound mushrooms, sliced
1 slice whole-wheat bread, crumbed
1 tablespoon chopped parsley

¼ teaspoon thyme
⅛ teaspoon salt
1 8-ounce can crushed pineapple,
    well drained; reserve syrup

Remove all but 1 tablespoon fat from frying pan in which chicken was cooked. In same pan sauté onion until tender. Add mushrooms; sauté lightly. Stir in bread crumbs, parsley, thyme, ⅛ teaspoon salt, and pineapple. Remove from heat; set aside while making sauce.

sauce

3 tablespoons butter or margarine
3 tablespoons all-purpose flour
Reserved pineapple syrup plus
    water to equal 3 cups liquid
1 cup nonfat dry milk powder
1 teaspoon salt

2 egg yolks, beaten
½ cup all-purpose whipping
    cream, whipped
3 tablespoons grated Parmesan cheese

1 tablespoon chopped parsley

Melt 3 tablespoons butter in separate saucepan. Remove from heat; stir in flour. Add liquid and dry milk powder. Cook, stirring, over medium heat until slightly thickened. Add 1 teaspoon salt. Stir small amount hot mixture into egg yolks, then add egg-yolk mixture slowly to hot mixture in saucepan while stirring. Stir and cook 2 to 3 minutes. Remove from heat. Fold in whipped cream.

Divide dressing mixture equally on tops of chicken breasts. Pour sauce over chicken, dressing, and noodles. Sprinkle with cheese and parsley. Place under broiler until browned.

sweet-and-sour chicken

Yield: 4 servings

    2 tablespoons soy sauce
    1 tablespoon cornstarch
    2 whole chicken breasts, halved, skinned, boned, cut into bite-size cubes
    1 tablespoon vegetable oil
    1 cucumber, scored lengthwise with tines of fork, cut into bite-size cubes
    ½ cantaloupe, seeded, rinded, cut into bite-size pieces
    1 sweet red pepper (or green pepper), cubed

sweet-and-sour sauce

    2 tablespoons brown sugar
    2 tablespoons vinegar
    ½ cup pineapple juice (unsweetened)
    1 tablespoon cornstarch in 2 tablespoons cold water

    3 ounces blanched whole almonds

Combine soy sauce and cornstarch. Coat chicken pieces thoroughly.

Heat oil in large frypan (or wok); stir-fry chicken 3 to 4 minutes. Add cucumber, cantaloupe, and pepper.

Mix together sauce ingredients. Add to chicken mixture. Heat, stirring often, until sauce boils and ingredients are heated through. Add almonds. Serve at once.

sweet-and-sour chicken

chicken barley bake

Yield: 4 to 6 servings

> 2 cups chicken broth or bouillon
> ½ pound barley
> 3 tablespoons butter or margarine
> 1 small onion, chopped
> ½ pound mushrooms, sliced
> 1 cup bite-size pieces cooked chicken
> ½ cup plain yogurt
> ¾ cup shredded Monterey Jack cheese
> 2 tablespoons chopped parsley

Heat broth to boiling in large saucepan. Add barley; cover. Simmer about 45 minutes or until tender.

Meanwhile melt butter in frypan; sauté onion until transparent. Add mushrooms; sauté lightly just until juices appear. Remove from heat; set aside.

Combine chicken, yogurt, and ½ cup cheese.

When barley has finished cooking, remove from heat. Add mushroom and chicken mixtures. Transfer to large greased casserole dish. Sprinkle with remaining cheese and parsley. Bake in 350°F oven 50 minutes.

chicken livers with apples and onion

Yield: 4 servings

> ¾ pound chicken livers
> 3 tablespoons flour
> ½ teaspoon salt
> ¼ teaspoon pepper
> ⅛ teaspoon cayenne pepper
> 3 medium apples
> ¼ cup vegetable oil
> ¼ cup sugar
> 1 large onion, thinly sliced

Rinse livers; drain on paper towels. Coat livers evenly with mixture of flour, salt, pepper, and cayenne pepper; set aside.

Wash apples; remove cores. Cut into ½-inch slices, to form rings.

Heat 2 tablespoons oil in frypan over medium heat. Add sliced apples; cook until lightly brown. Turn slices carefully; sprinkle with sugar. Cook, uncovered, over low heat until tender. Remove from pan; reserve.

Heat remaining oil over low heat. Add livers and onion rings. Cook over medium heat, turning often to brown all sides. Transfer liver mixture to warm serving platter. Serve with apple rings.

tomatoes stuffed with chicken

Yield: 6 servings

½ teaspoon salt
¼ teaspoon tarragon
1 cup plain yogurt
1 can (8 ounces) crushed pineapple, drained
1½ cups diced cooked chicken
½ cup toasted slivered almonds
1 stalk celery, finely diced
6 tomatoes

To prepare dressing, stir salt and tarragon into yogurt; chill.

In separate bowl combine pineapple, chicken, almonds, and celery; chill.

Just before serving, stir dressing lightly into chicken mixture.

Cut tomatoes partially into sections; fill with salad. Garnish with parsley, if desired.

egg foo yung

Yield: 4 servings

1 small onion	2 eggs, slightly beaten
1 tomato	2 tablespoons vegetable oil
½ cup cooked chicken	1 cup sprouts (see Index, or buy
¼ cup canned sliced water chestnuts	bean sprouts)
3 scallions, thinly sliced	2 teaspoons sugar
2 tablespoons soy sauce	1½ teaspoons cornstarch
3 large mushrooms, sliced	¾ cup water

Peel onion. Cut in half lengthwise; cut halves into ½-inch-wide lengthwise strips.

Cut tomato in half and into thin lengthwise wedges.

Place chicken in bowl. Add water chestnuts, scallions, 1 tablespoon soy sauce, mushrooms, and eggs; mix together lightly.

Heat 1 tablespoon oil in small heavy frypan. Spoon about ¼ of egg mixture into frypan. Spread ¼ of sprouts, tomato slices, and ⅛ teaspoon sugar over egg mixture. Cook until "cake" is nicely browned on underside, about 3 minutes. Carefully turn with pancake turner; brown other side. Cook until edges are a little crisp. Remove cake; keep warm. Add more oil to frypan as necessary. Cook remaining cakes.

While cakes are cooking, mix cornstarch and 1½ teaspoons sugar in small saucepan. Add water gradually; blend until smooth. Heat to boiling. Add 1 tablespoon soy sauce; simmer 1 minute. Serve hot sauce on egg foo yung.

turkey-salad bake

Yield: 6 servings

pastry

> 1 cup whole-wheat pastry flour
> ¼ teaspoon salt
> 6 tablespoons butter or margarine, softened

Stir together flour and salt. Cut in butter with pastry blender until crumbly. With hands, pat dough firmly in bottom of 11¾ × 7½-inch baking dish. Bake at 400°F 5 minutes.

filling

> ¾ cup mayonnaise
> 2 teaspoons lemon juice
> ½ teaspoon poultry seasoning
> ½ teaspoon salt
> ⅛ teaspoon pepper
> 1 cup shredded cheddar cheese
> 1 cup slivered almonds
> 1 tablespoon all-purpose flour
> 2 cups fresh alfalfa sprouts
> 2 cups chopped cooked turkey
> 2 stalks celery, chopped
> 1 tablespoon chopped parsley

Combine mayonnaise, lemon juice, poultry seasoning, salt, and pepper.
Reserve ¼ cup each cheese and almonds. Toss remaining cheese with flour. Add to mayonnaise mixture along with remaining almonds. Add remaining ingredients except parsley and reserved cheese and almonds. Spoon evenly over crust. Top with cheese and almonds. Sprinkle with parsley. Bake at 400°F 25 to 30 minutes.

seafood

yogurt-sauced fish

Yield: 4 to 6 servings

yogurt sauce

> 1 cup plain yogurt
> 2 tablespoons all-purpose flour
> 2 teaspoons grated lemon rind
> 1 small onion, minced
> ¾ teaspoon salt

Blend yogurt, flour, lemon rind, onion and salt in small bowl.

fish

> 1½ pounds mild whitefish (whitefish, ocean perch, haddock, etc.)
> ¼ teaspoon paprika
> Dash freshly ground pepper

Place fish in shallow 2-quart baking dish; pour sauce over. Sprinkle paprika and pepper over sauce.

Bake at 350°F 20 to 30 minutes or just until tender. Do not overcook.

fish fillets on spinach

Yield: 6 servings

   1½ pounds fish fillets
   Juice of 1 lemon
   2 pounds fresh spinach
   2 tablespoons vegetable oil
   1 medium onion, chopped
   ½ teaspoon salt
   ⅛ teaspoon white pepper
   ½ teaspoon grated fresh nutmeg
   2 tomatoes
   ¼ cup grated mozzarella cheese

Wash fish; pat dry. Sprinkle with lemon juice; let stand 10 minutes.

Wash spinach well; chop coarsely.

Heat oil in frypan. Add onion; sauté until soft. Fry fish in pan with onion few minutes on each side, until golden brown. Remove fish and onion; reserve.

Add spinach to frypan; stir-fry 4 to 5 minutes.

Grease casserole dish. Add spinach. Arrange fish fillets on top of spinach; sprinkle with salt, pepper, and nutmeg. Place sliced tomatoes on top of fish. Sprinkle with cheese. Bake in preheated 350°F oven 15 minutes.

fish fillets on spinach

crab-stuffed green peppers

Yield: 4 servings

4 seeded green peppers
1 6½-ounce can crab meat, tendons removed, flaked
2 eggs, beaten
1 medium onion, minced
2 stalks celery, chopped
2 tablespoons butter or margarine
3 slices bacon, crisp-cooked, crumbled
1 cup whole-wheat bread crumbs (2 slices)
1 tablespoon toasted wheat germ
½ teaspoon salt
Dash of pepper

Cook peppers in boiling water until tender-crisp, about 5 minutes.
Combine crab meat and eggs in mixing bowl; set aside.
Fry onion and celery in butter until onion is tender. Stir in bacon, bread crumbs, wheat germ, salt, and pepper. Add to crab-meat mixture. Divide mixture equally to fill green peppers. Set stuffed peppers upright in flat baking dish; bake at 350°F 20 to 25 minutes.

riki's shrimp pie

Yield: 4 to 5 servings

2 tablespoons minced shallots or green onions
1 large clove garlic, crushed
¼ cup butter or margarine
1 cup sliced mushrooms
2 4½-ounce can tiny shrimp, drained
1 tablespoon chopped chives
2 tablespoons chopped parsley
Dash each salt and pepper
⅓ cup white wine
1 8-ounce package cream cheese, softened
1 cup sour cream
1 egg, beaten
Pastry for 9-inch Double Pie Crust (see Index)

Sauté shallots and garlic in butter. Add mushrooms; sauté 3 to 4 minutes. Stir in shrimp, chives, parsley, salt, and pepper. Add wine; stir-fry quickly over high heat until liquid has evaporated. Remove pan from heat; remove garlic clove.
Beat together cream cheese, sour cream, and egg in small bowl. Add to shrimp mixture.
Spoon into unbaked pie shell. Cover with pricked top crust. Bake at 375°F 1 hour.

shrimp with marinara sauce

Yield: 4 servings

>   1 quart water
>   ½ teaspoon salt
>   1 bay leaf
>   1 pound large shrimp

Bring water, salt, and bay leaf to boil in saucepan. Add shrimp; boil 5 minutes. Drain; cool. Peel and devein shrimp.

marinara sauce

>   2 tablespoons vegetable oil
>   1 clove garlic, minced
>   ½ small onion, chopped
>   2 cups canned pressed and drained whole or Italian tomatoes (reserve
>   ⅓ cup juice)
>   2 finely chopped anchovy fillets
>   ½ teaspoon sugar
>   ½ teaspoon oregano

Heat oil in frypan; sauté garlic and onion until tender. Slowly add tomatoes; break up pieces. Stir in ⅓ cup juice, anchovies, sugar, and oregano. Bring to boil; gently simmer, uncovered, 20 minutes. Stir occasionally.

Place shrimp in lightly greased au gratin dish. Top with sauce.

topping

>   3 tablespoons dry bread crumbs
>   2 tablespoons grated Parmesan cheese
>   1 tablespoon finely chopped parsley

Combine ingredients; sprinkle over sauce. Bake in preheated 425°F oven 12 to 15 minutes.

shrimp with marinara sauce

seafood stew

Yield: 4 to 6 servings

2½ tablespoons butter or margarine
1 small onion, chopped
2 stalks celery, including tops, chopped
1 large carrot, diced
1 cup water
1 8-ounce can minced clams, including juice
1 8-ounce can whole shelled baby clams, including juice
1 pound fish fillets, cut into bite-size pieces (ocean perch, haddock, sole, etc.)
1 cup nonfat dry milk powder
1 chicken bouillon cube
2 large potatoes, peeled, diced
¼ teaspoon salt
⅛ teaspoon pepper
Dash of celery salt

Melt butter in large saucepan. Sauté onion, celery, and carrot until onion is tender. Stir in water, clams, fish, milk powder, and bouillon. Add potatoes and seasonings; cover. Simmer over very low heat about 20 minutes or until potatoes are tender. Do not allow to boil.

bouillabaisse

bouillabaisse

Yield: 6 servings

sauce

2 tablespoons vegetable oil
2 onions, chopped, or 3 leeks, sliced
4 cloves garlic, crushed
2 fresh tomatoes, peeled, diced
3 tablespoons tomato paste
2 cups bottled clam juice
4 cups chicken bouillon
1 tablespoon salt
1/8 teaspoon pepper
1/4 teaspoon saffron
1/2 teaspoon thyme
1 bay leaf
6 sprigs parsley
Grated rind of 1 orange

Heat oil in large saucepan or Dutch oven. Sauté onions several minutes, until translucent. Add remaining sauce ingredients; simmer 45 minutes.

seafoods

1 2-pound lobster and/or other shellfish, such as clams, mussels (with shells), scallops, crab, or shrimp
2 pounds assorted whitefish fillets, such as sea bass, perch, cod, sole, flounder, or red snapper

Chopped parsley for garnish

Prepare seafoods. Place lobster in large kettle of boiling salted water 10 minutes. Break claws and tail from body; crack claws. Cut tail into 1-inch chunks. Remove black vein from tail pieces; leave shell on meat. Wash fish fillets; cut into 2-inch pieces.

Add lobster and firm-fleshed fish (sea bass, perch, etc.) to boiling sauce; boil rapidly 5 minutes. Add tender-fleshed fish, such as clams, scallops, sole, or cod; boil 5 minutes. Lift seafoods out as soon as cooked; keep warm in soup tureen or platter.

Boil liquid 10 minutes to reduce. Strain liquid through coarse sieve into tureen, mashing through some of vegetables. Garnish with parsley.

62

other main dishes

puffy cheese–sprout omelet

Yield: 4 to 6 servings

> 6 eggs, separated
> ¼ cup milk
> ½ teaspoon salt
> 1½ tablespoons butter or margarine
> 1 cup alfalfa sprouts
> 1½ cups grated cheddar cheese

Beat egg yolks until thick and lemon-colored. Beat in milk and salt.

Beat egg whites until stiff but not dry. Fold yolks into whites.

Heat butter in large ovenproof frying pan. Pour in egg mixture. Spread sprouts and cheese on top of mixture, no closer than 1 inch from sides of pan. Push lightly into omelet. Cook over low heat until puffed and set and edges are golden on bottom when lifted with knife (8 to 10 minutes). Place in 325°F oven until top is brown, about 10 minutes. Garnish with fresh parsley if desired.

eggplant–cheese patties

Yield: 4 to 5 patties

> 1 medium eggplant
> 2 eggs, beaten
> 1½ cups whole-wheat bread crumbs
> 1 cup grated cheddar cheese
> 2 tablespoons grated Parmesan cheese
> 2 tablespoons wheat germ
> 2 tablespoons minced onion
> ½ teaspoon celery salt
> ¼ teaspoon dry mustard
> ¼ teaspoon salt
> ⅛ teaspoon pepper
> Dash of garlic salt

Peel eggplant; cut into 1-inch cubes. Cook, covered, in boiling, salted water 5 to 6 minutes, until tender. Drain well; chop finely. Stir in remaining ingredients. Shape into patties. Fry in butter or oil on hot griddle until golden brown on each side.

cheese quiche

Yield: 4 servings

> 1 Single-Crust Pie Pastry, unbaked (use Whole-Wheat Pie Crust if desired; see Index)
> 4 slices bacon
> 3 eggs
> 1 cup milk
> 1 cup shredded Swiss cheese
> ¼ cup freshly grated Parmesan cheese
> ½ teaspoon salt
> ⅛ teaspoon white pepper

Roll out pastry on floured board to ⅛ inch thick; fit into 9-inch quiche or pie pan.

Cook bacon until crisp; drain. Crumble; place in pie shell.

Combine eggs, milk, cheeses, and seasonings. Pour into pastry-lined pan. Bake in preheated 375°F oven 25 minutes or until knife inserted in custard comes out clean.

Serve quiche hot, warm, or cold.

eggplant parmesan

Yield: 6 servings

> 1 medium eggplant
> ½ teaspoon salt
> 2 egg whites, slightly beaten
> ¼ cup bread crumbs
> 3 tablespoons vegetable oil
> 2 tomatoes, thinly sliced
> ½ pound fresh mushrooms, sliced
> 1 cup tomato sauce
> ½ pound sliced mozzarella cheese

Peel eggplant; cut into ½-inch slices. Sprinkle with salt; let stand 1 hour. Rinse with cold water. Pound eggplant slices to ¼ inch thick. (Use meat mallet or edge of saucer.) Dip slices in egg whites, then in bread crumbs. Sauté in hot oil; drain on paper towels. Arrange eggplant in bottom of ovenproof baking dish. Place layer of tomato slices on eggplant, followed by layer of mushrooms. Pour tomato sauce over all; arrange cheese on top. Bake at 450°F 20 minutes. If desired, brown cheese under broiler a minute or 2 at end of cooking time.

cheese quiche

sherman's new england baked beans

Yield: 8 servings

1 pound dry beans
     (navy, pea, or soldier)
6 cups cold water
¼ pound salt pork,
     cut into ½-inch pieces
1½ teaspoons salt
⅓ cup brown sugar
¼ cup molasses
1 tablespoon vinegar
¾ teaspoon dry mustard
1 small onion, minced

sherman's new england baked beans

Rinse beans. In 3-quart saucepan or large pot add beans to cold water. Bring to boil; simmer 5 minutes. Remove from heat; cover. Let stand 1 hour. (This method saves soaking beans overnight.)

Drain beans; reserve liquid. Place beans and salt pork into 2-quart greased casserole or bean pot.

Make sauce by combining 2½ cups bean liquid and remaining ingredients. Pour liquid over beans; cover. Bake at 300°F 8 to 10 hours. Add more bean liquid or hot water when needed. Remove cover ½ hour before serving if browner beans are desired.

corn–cheese quiche

Yield: 6 servings

1 Single Pie Crust pastry, unbaked (see Index)
3 ears corn (or about 1 cup kernels)
4 eggs
1 cup milk
½ cup light (table) cream
½ cup freshly grated Parmesan cheese
2 tablespoons finely chopped onion
1 teaspoon salt
¼ teaspoon pepper
6 slices bacon
Parsley for garnish

Roll out pastry on floured board to ⅛ inch thick; fit into 9-inch quiche or pie pan.

Cut kernels off corncobs; reserve.

Beat eggs in large mixing bowl. Stir in milk, cream, cheese, onion, salt, and pepper; mix well. Add corn. Pour into pie shell. Bake in preheated 375°F oven 20 minutes.

Meanwhile fry bacon until almost done; drain on paper towels. Arrange bacon on top of pie; bake 10 minutes or until knife inserted in custard comes out clean.

Garnish quiche with parsley; serve hot.

corn–cheese quiche

soybeans polynesian

For added flavor, prepare this dish several hours before the meal. Refrigerate while soybeans "marinate" in sauce. Reheat and serve.

Yield: 3 to 4 servings

1 green sweet pepper, seeded, cut into ½-inch chunks
1 red sweet pepper, seeded, cut into ½-inch chunks
1 tablespoon vegetable oil
1 8-ounce can pineapple chunks, drained; reserve juice
1½ cups cooked soybeans
Juice from pineapple chunks
¼ cup catsup
2 teaspoons cider vinegar
1 tablespoon soy sauce
2 tablespoons brown sugar
¼ teaspoon salt (optional)

Sauté peppers in oil 2 to 3 minutes; remove from heat. Add pineapple and soybeans.

Combine pineapple juice, catsup, vinegar, soy sauce, brown sugar, and salt. Pour over soybean mixture. Cook, stirring, over medium-high heat until mixture thickens somewhat and coats ingredients, about 5 to 8 minutes.

Serve soybeans with rice.

slow-cooker soybean spaghetti sauce

Yield: About 2 quarts

¼ cup vegetable oil
3 medium onions, chopped
2 stalks celery including leaves, chopped
3 cloves garlic, minced
¼ cup chopped fresh parsley
2 beef bouillon cubes, crumbled
⅓ cup red wine
1 12-ounce can tomato paste
2 cups cooked soybeans
1 28-ounce can crushed tomatoes
1 8-ounce can tomato sauce

½ cup water
1 teaspoon Italian seasoning
1 teaspoon oregano
1 teaspoon basil
¼ teaspoon thyme
1 tablespoon brown sugar
½ teaspoon celery salt
1 teaspoon salt
¼ teaspoon pepper
1 bay leaf

Heat oil in large frying pan. Sauté onions, celery, garlic, parsley, and bouillon cubes until vegetables are tender. Add wine, tomato paste, and soybeans. Cook, stirring, 2 to 3 minutes. Transfer to slow cooker. Add remaining ingredients. Cook on low 6 to 8 hours.

Serve sauce over cooked spaghetti. Pass grated Parmesan cheese.

For flavor variation, add 1 8-ounce can mushrooms and 1 cup chopped green pepper to sauce before cooking.

spinach soufflé

Yield: 4 servings

　　5 tablespoons butter or margarine
　　1 tablespoon minced shallots or green onions
　　¾ cup chopped frozen spinach, thawed
　　Dash of nutmeg
　　3 tablespoons flour
　　1 cup milk
　　½ teaspoon salt
　　Dash of pepper
　　4 eggs, separated
　　¼ teaspoon cream of tartar
　　1 tablespoon Parmesan cheese or bread crumbs

Melt 1 tablespoon butter in small pan. Sauté shallots several minutes, until tender. Add spinach; cook few minutes to remove moisture. Add nutmeg; set aside.

Melt 3 tablespoons butter in 1-quart saucepan. Stir in flour; cook several minutes. Add milk all at once. Add salt and pepper; cook and stir over medium heat until sauce thickens. Stir in spinach. Cool sauce slightly, then add egg yolks; mix well.

Beat egg whites in medium-size bowl until frothy. Beat in cream of tartar; beat until soft peaks form. Stir ¼ of egg whites into spinach mixture. Gently fold in remaining whites.

Prepare 1½- or 2-quart soufflé dish by greasing with 1 tablespoon butter and dusting with cheese. Pour soufflé into dish. Bake in preheated 375°F oven 25 to 30 minutes. Soufflé is done when golden, puffed, and somewhat dry, not shiny.

Serve soufflé at once, with sauce if desired.

cheesy summer-squash "pizza"

Yield: 4 servings

2½ cups grated yellow summer squash	1 small onion, finely chopped
¾ cup grated cheddar cheese	½ cup tomato sauce
1 egg, beaten	1 teaspoon Italian seasoning
½ teaspoon salt	Dash of pepper
1 tablespoon butter or margarine	¼ cup grated Parmesan cheese
½ cup sliced mushrooms	1 cup grated mozzarella cheese
½ pound lean ground beef	1 tablespoon chopped fresh parsley

Combine squash, cheese, egg, and salt. Press into 9-inch pie pan. Bake 10 minutes in 400°F oven. Let cool while preparing remaining ingredients.

Melt butter in frying pan; lightly sauté mushrooms 2 to 3 minutes. Remove from pan; set aside.

In same pan brown ground beef and onion. Add tomato sauce, Italian seasoning, ¼ teaspoon salt, and pepper. Simmer 5 minutes. Spread mixture over squash "crust." Arrange mushroom slices over sauce. Top with cheeses and parsley. Bake at 400°F 25 minutes or until browned. Let cool 5 minutes before slicing.

italian zucchini omelet

Yield: 2 servings

½ cup thinly sliced zucchini
2 slices onion
1 tablespoon vegetable oil
4 eggs
4 tablespoons water
¼ teaspoon basil
½ teaspoon salt
Dash of pepper
1 tablespoon butter or margarine
3 tablespoons diced fresh tomato
2 tablespoons grated Parmesan cheese

italian zucchini omelet

In medium ovenproof frypan sauté zucchini and onion in oil until tender. Remove vegetables with slotted spoon; reserve vegetables and oil.

Combine eggs, water, basil, salt, and pepper. Stir in cooked vegetables.

Heat butter in pan with reserved oil until hot enough to sizzle a drop of water. Pour egg mixture into hot pan. Mixture will start to set immediately. Sprinkle tomato and cheese over top of omelet. With fork, lightly pull cooked edge away from side of pan, so uncooked portions flow to bottom. When only top is uncooked, place pan 4 to 6 inches from broiler flame about 2 minutes to melt cheese and brown top. Serve at once.

brown-rice and cheese bake

Yield: 6 to 8 servings

3 cups cooked brown rice
1 tablespoon vegetable oil
½ cup chopped onion
6 ounces Swiss cheese, grated
½ cup sesame seeds
1 egg, beaten
1 cup milk
⅛ cup chopped parsley
Parsley sprigs to garnish

Sauté onion in hot oil until soft.

Combine all ingredients; place in greased casserole. Bake in preheated 350°F oven 40 minutes or until hot and slightly brown on top. Garnish with parsley sprigs.

vegetables

asparagus with bean sprouts

Yield: 4 to 5 servings

> 2 teaspoons butter or margarine
> 1 tablespoon vegetable oil
> ¼ cup cashew nuts
> ½ small onion, chopped
> 1 clove garlic, minced
> 1 10-ounce package frozen cut asparagus
> ¼ teaspoon salt
> ¼ teaspoon ground ginger
> 1 cup fresh mung-bean sprouts

Melt butter and oil in skillet. Add cashews; toast, stirring, until golden. Remove nuts; set aside.

Add onion and garlic to butter remaining in pan. Cook until onion is transparent. Stir in asparagus and seasonings; cover. Cook, stirring frequently, until asparagus is crisp-tender, about 7 to 10 minutes. Stir in sprouts and cashews. Stir-fry just until sprouts are hot. Remove from heat; serve.

green beans with mushroom sauce

Yield: 4 servings

> 3 cups French-style green beans

mushroom sauce

> 2 cups sliced mushrooms
> 3 tablespoons butter or margarine
> 2 teaspoons all-purpose flour
> ¼ teaspoon salt
> Pepper to taste
> ½ cup plain yogurt

Cook beans in boiling water until tender.

Sauté mushrooms in butter until just soft. Stir in flour, salt, and pepper; cook and stir until flour absorbs mushroom juices and thickens. Remove from heat; stir in yogurt. Add beans; warm slightly, but *do not boil.*

green beans with water chestnuts and sunflower seeds

Yield: 4 to 5 servings

3 tablespoons sunflower seeds
1 tablespoon butter or margarine
1 tablespoon vegetable oil
½ small onion, chopped
1 clove garlic
1 9-ounce package frozen French-style green beans, thawed
½ teaspoon salt
½ teaspoon dry mustard
Dash of pepper
½ cup thinly sliced water chestnuts

Stir-fry sunflower seeds in butter and oil in frying pan until golden brown. Remove with slotted spoon; set aside.

Add onion and garlic to remaining butter–oil mixture. Cook, stirring, until onion is soft. Remove garlic clove. Add beans, salt, mustard, and pepper to onion in pan. Stir-fry 3 to 4 minutes. Add water chestnuts; partially cover. Cook over medium heat, stirring frequently, 3 to 5 minutes, until beans are tender. Stir in sunflower seeds.

green beans with yogurt–horseradish sauce

Yield: 6 servings

2 10-ounce packages frozen French-style green beans, cooked
2 teaspoons butter or margarine

yogurt–horseradish sauce

1 cup plain yogurt
1 tablespoon prepared horseradish
¼ teaspoon dillweed
⅛ teaspoon freshly ground pepper

Stir butter into hot cooked beans.
Combine remaining ingredients. Pour over hot beans. Toss lightly.

broccoli casserole

Yield: 6 servings

2 pounds fresh broccoli (or 1 10-ounce package frozen broccoli)
1½ cups milk
3 eggs, beaten
½ teaspoon salt
¼ teaspoon pepper
½ teaspoon nutmeg
¾ cup grated cheddar cheese

Cut fresh broccoli into spears. Peel skins off stalks; slice stalks lengthwise if thick. Steam or boil broccoli (fresh or frozen) until almost tender. Drain; reserve.

Meanwhile heat milk to lukewarm in medium saucepan. Add eggs, salt, pepper, nutmeg, and cheese. Beating constantly, heat just enough to melt cheese and blend all ingredients. Pour into greased baking dish. Add broccoli. Bake in preheated 350°F oven 30 to 40 minutes or until knife inserted in center comes clean. Serve immediately.

broccoli casserole

wheat 'n ginger broccoli

Yield: 4 to 6 servings

> ¼ cup butter or margarine
> 1 clove garlic, minced
> ½ teaspoon salt
> ½ teaspoon ground ginger
> 2 tablespoons wheat germ
> 3 cups fresh broccoli, cut into bite-size pieces, cooked until tender-crisp

Melt butter in frying pan; sauté garlic until tender. Add salt, ginger, and wheat germ; stir-fry quickly until well mixed and wheat germ is just browned, being careful not to burn mixture. Add broccoli; stir to coat. Heat through.

cheese-sauced brussels sprouts

Yield: 6 to 8 servings

> 2 10-ounce packages frozen brussels sprouts (or 4 cups fresh)
> 3 tablespoons butter or margarine
> 2 medium onions, chopped
> 3 stalks celery, chopped
> 3½ tablespoons all-purpose flour
> Water (see directions)
> ½ cup nonfat dry milk powder
> ½ teaspoon salt
> ½ teaspoon ground nutmeg
> 1½ cups shredded cheddar cheese
> 1 cup buttered whole-wheat bread crumbs (2 slices, buttered)

Cook brussels sprouts in boiling water 5 to 8 minutes or until just tender. Drain; reserve 1⅔ cups cooking water. (Add more water to measure 1⅔ cups if not enough.) Cut brussels sprouts into halves.

Heat butter in large frypan; sauté onions until golden. Add celery; cook, stirring, about 5 minutes. Remove from heat; stir in flour. Add 1⅔ cups brussels sprouts water, dry milk, salt, and nutmeg. Cook, stirring, over medium heat until thickened. Add 1 cup cheese; stir until melted. Add brussels sprouts. Pour into 2-quart casserole dish. Top with remaining cheese and bread crumbs. Bake in 350°F oven 20 to 25 minutes, until browned and bubbly.

red cabbage

Yield: 4 servings

2 tablespoons vegetable oil
2 small onions, sliced
2 pounds red cabbage, shredded
2 tablespoons vinegar
Salt to taste
1 teaspoon sugar

1 large tart apple, peeled, cored, finely chopped, or
½ cup applesauce
2-ounce piece salt pork
½ cup red wine
½ cup hot beef broth

Heat oil in Dutch oven; sauté onions 3 minutes. Add cabbage; immediately pour vinegar over cabbage to prevent it from losing its red color. Sprinkle with salt and sugar. Add apple and salt pork. Pour in red wine and broth; cover. Simmer 45 to 60 minutes. Cabbage should be just tender, not soft. Shortly before end of cooking time, remove salt pork; cube and return it to cabbage if desired. Correct seasonings; serve.

red cabbage

sweet-and-sour celery

sweet-and-sour celery

Yield: 6 servings

 1 bunch fresh celery
 4 slices bacon
 1 small onion, sliced into rings
 ¼ cup white vinegar
 1 tablespoon sugar
 ¼ teaspoon salt
 ¼ teaspoon white pepper

Wash and trim celery; cut stalks into 1-inch diagonal pieces.

Fry bacon in large frypan until crisp. Drain on paper towels. Drain bacon fat except 2 tablespoons.

Add celery and onion to hot bacon fat; sauté 6 to 8 minutes, stirring often. Reduce heat; cover. Cook 10 to 12 minutes or until vegetables are just tender. Stir in vinegar, sugar, salt, and pepper; heat through.

Place mixture in serving dish; crumble bacon over top.

maple-sautéed carrots

Yield: 4 to 5 servings

 4 cups carrots, cut into 1½-inch strips, julienne-style (about 1 pound)
 ¼ cup butter or margarine
 ½ teaspoon cornstarch
 ¼ cup pure maple syrup
 1 teaspoon dry mustard
 ¾ teaspoon salt

Sauté carrots in butter 6 to 8 minutes, until tender-crisp.

Blend cornstarch with maple syrup until smooth. Stir syrup, mustard, and salt into carrots. Stir-fry about 5 minutes, until carrots are just tender. (If more cooking is desired, cover and simmer 5 more minutes.)

sesame-sautéed carrots

Yield: 5 to 6 servings

 3 tablespoons sesame seeds
 2½ tablespoons vegetable oil
 4 cups grated carrots
 Salt to taste

Sauté sesame seeds in oil until brown. Add carrots; stir-fry quickly 1 to 2 minutes. Salt and serve.

eggplant supreme

Yield: 4 to 6 servings

> 1 large eggplant, peeled, cut into 1-inch cubes
> 1 egg, beaten
> ⅔ cup milk
> ¾ cup shredded cheddar cheese
> 1 small onion, chopped
> 2 slices whole-wheat bread, crumbled
> 4 teaspoons butter or margarine
> ½ teaspoon salt
> ¼ cup toasted wheat germ
> ¼ cup butter-cracker crumbs

Cook eggplant in boiling salted water just until soft, about 7 to 9 minutes.
Combine egg, milk, cheese, onion, bread crumbs, butter, and salt.
When finished cooking, drain eggplant. Add to egg–cheese mixture. Carefully stir ingredients together until butter has melted. Pour into greased 1½-quart casserole dish.
Combine wheat germ and crumbs; sprinkle on top of eggplant mixture. Bake at 350°F 50 to 60 minutes.

honey-buttered parsnips

Yield: 4 servings

> 1½ pounds parsnips, peeled, sliced
> 3 tablespoons butter or margarine
> 3 tablespoons honey
> Dash of salt

Cook parsnips in boiling water until tender-crisp, about 5 minutes; drain. Sauté in butter until golden brown. Drizzle with honey; stir just to coat. Salt to taste.

minted peas

Yield: 3 to 4 servings

> 2 tablespoons butter or margarine
> 2 tablespoons diced fresh mint leaves
> ¼ teaspoon salt
> 1 10-ounce package frozen peas, cooked

Melt butter; add mint leaves. Let set 15 minutes to develop flavor. Add salt; rewarm butter until hot.
Cook peas in boiling water 2 to 3 minutes; drain. Pour mint butter over peas.

mushrooms baked in cheese sauce

Yield: 4 servings

8 large mushrooms
1 tablespoon vegetable oil

cheese sauce

2 tablespoons butter or margarine
2 tablespoons flour
¼ teaspoon salt
1 cup milk
1 cup freshly grated Parmesan cheese
2 tablespoons finely minced scallions
¾ cup fine bread crumbs

Remove stems from mushrooms. Reserve caps; chop stems. Sauté chopped mushrooms in hot oil until most fat is absorbed. Set aside.

Make sauce. Melt butter in saucepan over low heat. Blend in flour and salt; stir to break up lumps. Add milk; heat, stirring constantly, until mixture is thick and bubbling. Add ¾ cup cheese; stir to melt. Add scallions and chopped mushrooms.

Arrange mushroom caps, round-side-down, in shallow baking dish. Pour Cheese Sauce over; sprinkle crumbs on top. Sprinkle remaining cheese evenly over bread crumbs. Bake in preheated 350°F oven 20 minutes or until topping is browned. (After baking, if darker browning is desired, place under broiler 2 to 3 minutes.)

mushrooms baked in cheese sauce

pepper pot

Yield: 4 to 6 servings

2 red sweet peppers
2 green sweet peppers
⅓ cup butter or margarine

4 onions, peeled, cut into wedges
6 tomatoes, cored, cut into wedges
Salt and pepper to taste

Remove tops, seeds, and membranes from peppers; slice into rings.

Melt butter in heavy frypan. Add peppers and onions. Sauté over medium heat about 10 minutes, stirring often. Add tomatoes; season to taste. Cook 10 minutes, stirring frequently. Serve hot.

This vegetable dish also freezes well.

creamy dilled potatoes

Yield: 5 to 6 servings

1 tablespoon butter or margarine
1 tablespoon all-purpose flour
¾ teaspoon salt
¼ teaspoon dried dillweed
1 cup milk

½ cup mayonnaise
3 tablespoons minced green onions
4 cups diced cooked potatoes (5 to 6 potatoes)
Paprika

Melt butter in medium saucepan. Blend in flour, salt, and dillweed. Add milk; cook, stirring, over low heat until mixture thickens. Blend in mayonnaise and onions; stir until smooth.

In large casserole alternate layers of cooked potatoes and sauce, beginning with potatoes and ending with sauce. Sprinkle with paprika. Bake in 350°F oven about 15 minutes, until warmed through and bubbly.

hawaiian sweet potatoes

Yield: 6 servings

1½ cups canned sweet potatoes plus
    3 tablespoons juice
1 tablespoon butter or margarine
½ teaspoon salt
¼ teaspoon pepper

¼ teaspoon nutmeg
¼ teaspoon cinnamon
1 tablespoon brown sugar
¾ cup crushed cereal flakes
6 pineapple slices

Combine sweet potatoes, juice, butter, salt, pepper, nutmeg, cinnamon, and brown sugar; mix until well blended.

Crush cereal flakes in plastic bag or between waxed paper. Drop ⅓ to ½ cup sweet-potato mixture onto waxed paper containing crushed cereal flakes; roll into ball. Place ball on pineapple slice in greased baking pan. Repeat potato-ball and pineapple procedure until all are prepared. Heat at 350°F 20 minutes.

ratatouille

Yield: 8 to 10 servings

1 medium eggplant
1 tablespoon salt
¼ cup olive or vegetable oil
2 large onions, sliced
3 cloves garlic, crushed
1 medium red pepper (optional),
    cored, cut into cubes
1 medium green pepper,
    cored, cut into cubes
4 medium zucchini,
    sliced ¾ inch thick

3 medium tomatoes, peeled, seeded,
    cut into coarse cubes
¼ teaspoon salt
Freshly ground pepper to taste
¼ teaspoon thyme
¼ teaspoon oregano
1 bay leaf
2 tablespoons chopped
    fresh parsley

Cut eggplant into ½-inch-thick slices, then into chunks. Sprinkle with 1 tablespoon salt; let stand 30 minutes, then dry thoroughly.

Heat oil in large frying pan. Sauté onions and garlic 2 minutes. Add peppers; cook 2 minutes. Add eggplant; brown lightly on both sides (about 3 minutes). Add zucchini, tomatoes, and seasonings, except parsley. Simmer gently, uncovered, 30 to 40 minutes, until all vegetables are just tender. Baste vegetables often; do not scorch. Cover; reduce heat if necessary. Remove bay leaf; chill.

Garnish casserole with parsley. Serve hot or cold.

apple–onion acorn squash

Yield: 6 servings

3 large acorn squash
4 medium onions, thinly sliced
¼ cup butter or margarine
4 medium red apples, cored, cut into 12 wedges each
Dash of salt
2½ tablespoons packed brown sugar

Wash squash; cut into halves; remove seeds. Place cut-side-down in shallow baking dish containing a little water. Bake in 375°F oven 20 minutes.

While squash are baking, sauté onions in butter until soft, about 5 minutes. Add apples; cook until apples are tender, about 7 to 9 minutes. Salt to taste. Stir in brown sugar.

Remove squash from oven. Turn right-side-up. Stuff squash halves with apple–onion mixture. Return to oven (*without* water in pan); bake 25 to 30 minutes, until squash are tender.

ratatouille

stuffed acorn squash

Yield: 4 servings

> 2 acorn squash, halved, seeded
> 3 tablespoons butter or margarine, melted
> 1 cup grated carrot
> ½ cup chopped pitted prunes
> ½ cup chopped dates
> ¼ teaspoon nutmeg

Place squash cut-side-down in baking pan with small amount of water. Bake at 350°F 30 minutes.

Combine remaining ingredients. Turn squash cut-side-up; fill with prune–date mixture. Bake 25 to 30 minutes or until squash is tender.

81

zucchini and tomato casserole

Yield: 4 servings

>   4 tablespoons vegetable oil
>   1 small onion, chopped
>   ½ clove garlic, minced
>   2 zucchini squash, sliced
>   2 tomatoes, peeled, or 1 cup canned tomatoes
>   ½ teaspoon salt
>   ½ teaspoon basil
>   ¼ teaspoon black pepper
>   2 tablespoons grated Parmesan cheese

Heat oil in heavy frypan; sauté onion and garlic. Stir in zucchini; cover. Cook until vegetables are tender. Add tomatoes, salt, basil, and pepper. Cook, uncovered, until mixture is well-blended, about 10 minutes. Sprinkle with cheese. Place under broiler a few minutes to brown top.

stuffed zucchini and tomatoes

Yield: 8 servings

>   4 medium zucchini
>   ½ cup water
>   2 cups fine bread crumbs
>   1/8 teaspoon oregano
>   1/3 cup butter or margarine, softened
>   1 small garlic clove, mashed through press
>   ¼ teaspoon salt
>
>   ¼ cup shredded Swiss cheese
>   ¼ cup freshly grated Parmesan cheese
>   4 firm ripe tomatoes
>   ½ teaspoon minced scallions
>   2 teaspoons finely chopped fresh parsley
>   ½ teaspoon dried tarragon
>   3 tablespoons butter or margarine, melted

Trim ends of zucchini; cut in half lengthwise. Place zucchini halves, cut-side-down, in large skillet. Add water; cover. Cook over low heat 10 minutes. Remove; cool. Carefully scoop pulp from centers into bowl. Drain off water from pulp. Mash pulp with fork; add *half* of following combined ingredients: bread crumbs, oregano, softened butter, garlic, salt, and Swiss cheese. Blend thoroughly. Spoon into squash shells; sprinkle tops with half the Parmesan cheese. Place filled squash in large shallow baking pan.

Cut tomatoes in half crosswise; scoop out centers. Drain tomato shells by turning cut-side-down. Combine tomato pulp and stuffing ingredients remaining from above. Spoon into shells; sprinkle tops with remaining Parmesan cheese. Place tomato halves in pan with zucchini. Sprinkle minced scallions, parsley, and tarragon on tops. Drizzle small amount melted butter over each stuffed vegetable. Bake in preheated 375°F oven 15 minutes or until stuffing bubbles. Place under broiler about 3 minutes to brown tops. Serve hot.

zucchini and cheese bake

Yield: 4 servings

2 medium zucchini squash, sliced
1 small onion, chopped
2 tablespoons vegetable oil

½ pound cottage cheese
½ teaspoon basil
2 tablespoons Parmesan cheese

Sauté zucchini and onion in hot oil; drain.
Puree cottage cheese and basil in blender.
Alternate layers of cottage cheese and zucchini in greased ovenproof casserole
dish. Sprinkle Parmesan cheese on top. Bake, uncovered, at 350°F 20 to 25 minutes.

stuffed zucchini and tomatoes

acorn squash with applesauce filling

Yield: 4 servings

> **2 acorn squash, cut in half**
> **1 cup unsweetened applesauce**
> **2 teaspoons brown sugar**
> **2 tablespoons raisins**
> **2 teaspoons butter or margarine**

Preheat oven to 400°F.

Remove seeds from squash; place halves cut-side-down in shallow baking pan. Add water to cover ½ inch of squash. Bake 50 to 60 minutes or until tender. Turn squash over. Fill each cavity with mixture of applesauce, brown sugar, and raisins. Dot with margarine. Bake 15 to 20 minutes or until applesauce bubbles.

polynesian vegetable stir-fry

Yield: 4 to 5 servings

> **1 tablespoon vegetable oil**
> **1 tablespoon butter or margarine**
> **¼ cup chopped onions**
> **1 cup diagonally sliced carrots**
> **½ teaspoon salt**
> **¼ teaspoon nutmeg**
> **¼ teaspoon ginger**
> **1 cup sliced celery**
> **1½ cups sliced mushrooms**
> **¼ cup cashew nuts (unsalted)**
> **¼ cup well-drained crushed pineapple**
> **¼ cup chopped dates**

Prepare all ingredients.

Melt oil and butter in frying pan. When very hot, cook onions, carrots, salt, nutmeg, and ginger over medium-high heat 1 to 2 minutes, stirring constantly. Add celery; stir-fry 1 to 2 minutes. Repeat, adding mushrooms. Stir in nuts, pineapple, and dates. Stir-fry briefly until heated through.

salads

starting sprouts

Yield: Approximately 1 quart

materials needed

> **Seeds for sprouting**
> **1 wide-mouth quart glass jar**
> **Clean cheesecloth or nylon stocking to fit over mouth of jar**
> **Rubber band or screw-top ring to fit jar mouth**

Place 2 tablespoons seeds in clean jar. Place cheesecloth over mouth of jar. Stretch tightly; fasten with rubber band or screw-top ring. Fill jar half-full with lukewarm water. Let stand overnight.

Next morning pour out water. Rinse 2 or 3 times with fresh lukewarm water; drain well. Place jar on its side in dark cupboard, shaking gently to distribute seeds along side of jar.

Remove jar from cupboard 2 or 3 times a day; repeat rinsing procedure. (Mealtimes are good times to remember to rinse seeds.) Drain well each time; place jar back on its side in dark cupboard.

After rinsing on morning of third or fourth day (depending on type of seed and length of sprouts), drain; place jar on sunny windowsill several hours, until sprouts turn green.

Remove cheesecloth. Fill jar to overflowing with fresh water. Hold sprouts in place with hands while many seed coats wash away; drain well. Store in refrigerator like lettuce. Use within 1 week.

banana waldorf salad

Yield: 4 servings

> **3 medium red apples, cored,**
>   **cut into ½-inch pieces**
> **1 banana, peeled, diced**
> **1 stalk celery, diced**
> **¼ cup coarsely chopped walnuts**

> **⅓ cup chopped dates or pitted prunes**
> **3 tablespoons mayonnaise**
> **1 teaspoon honey**
> **Dash of lemon juice**

Combine all ingredients; toss lightly. Serve in lettuce cups.

85

cabbage salad

Yield: 6 to 8 servings

banana salad dressing

> 1 ripe banana, mashed
> ½ teaspoon lemon juice
> 2 tablespoons honey
> ¼ cup mayonnaise or salad dressing
> ¼ cup plain yogurt

Beat banana with fork until smooth. Add lemon juice. Stir in honey, mayonnaise, and yogurt.

> 3 cups chopped or shredded cabbage
> 1 cup chopped celery
> ½ cup raisins
> ½ cup chopped peanuts

Combine cabbage, celery, raisins, and peanuts. Pour dressing over cabbage mixture. Toss to coat.

apple cabbage salad

Yield: 6 to 8 servings

yogurt salad dressing

> 1 tablespoon cider vinegar
> 1 teaspoon caraway seeds
> 1 teaspoon prepared mustard
> ½ teaspoon salt
> ⅛ teaspoon garlic salt
> 1 cup plain yogurt

Combine vinegar and spices. Fold into yogurt; cover. Chill several hours.

> 2 medium red apples, unpeeled, chopped coarsely
> 1 teaspoon lemon juice
> 2 cups shredded green cabbage
> 2 cups shredded red cabbage
> ¾ cup finely chopped celery

Coat apples with lemon juice. When ready to serve, mix dressing with apples, cabbages, and celery.

cabbage fruit salad with sour-cream dressing

Yield: 4 servings

> 2 cups shredded raw cabbage
> 1 red apple, diced (do not peel)
> 1 tablespoon lemon juice
> ½ cup raisins

Prepare cabbage and apple. Use 1 tablespoon lemon juice to wet diced apples to prevent darkening. Toss cabbage, apples, and raisins.

sour-cream salad dressing

> ¼ cup pineapple juice
> 1½ teaspoons lemon juice
> ¼ teaspoon salt
> 1 tablespoon sugar
> ½ cup sour cream

Mix juices, salt, and sugar. Add sour cream; stir until smooth.
Add dressing to salad; chill.

fruited chicken salad

Yield: 4 to 6 servings

> 4 cups cubed cooked chicken
> 1½ cups sliced celery
> 1 cup halved seedless green grapes
> 1 cup pineapple chunks, well drained, cut into ½-inch cubes
> 1 cup cashew nuts

Combine chicken, celery, grapes, pineapple, and ¾ cup cashew nuts in large bowl. Set aside.

salad dressing

> 1 cup mayonnaise
> 2 teaspoons lemon juice
> ½ teaspoon salt
> Dash of pepper
> ½ cup plain yogurt

Combine dressing ingredients in separate bowl; gently stir in yogurt.
Add dressing to chicken mixture; toss lightly. Chill thoroughly.
To serve, arrange on bed of lettuce. Coarsely chop remaining ¼ cup cashew nuts; sprinkle on top of salad. For added color, orange slices or unpeeled apple wedges can be arranged around edges of salad.

chef's salad

Yield: 4 servings

> ½ head Boston lettuce
> 1 large tomato, cut into eighths
> ½ cucumber, thinly sliced
> 1 small onion, grated
> ½ green pepper, cut into thin strips

Wash lettuce; tear into bite-size pieces. Arrange on salad platter with tomato, cucumber, onion, and green pepper. Cover; refrigerate while preparing dressing and remaining ingredients.

salad dressing

> ½ cup plain yogurt
> 1 tablespoon lemon juice
> ½ teaspoon salt
> ⅛ teaspoon white pepper
> 1 clove garlic, minced
> 1 teaspoon chopped parsley
> 1 teaspoon dried dill

Blend yogurt with lemon juice; season with salt, pepper, garlic, parsley, and dill.

Pour dressing over salad greens.

> ½ cup cooked chicken, cut into julienne strips
> ½ cup chopped cooked ham
> ¼ cup mozzarella cheese, cut into julienne strips
> 2 sardines, drained, cut in half lengthwise
> 3 stuffed green olives, sliced

Arrange meats, cheese, and sardines on top of salad. Garnish with sliced olives.

simple soybean salad

Yield: 4 main-dish servings

> 3 cups cooked, drained soybeans
> ¼ cup minced onion
> 1⅓ cups crumbled feta cheese (about 10 ounces)
> ⅔ cup mayonnaise (do not use salad dressing)
> Dash of freshly ground pepper

Combine all ingredients; chill several hours.
Serve salad on crisp lettuce leaves.

chef's salad

feta-cheese salad

Yield: 4 servings

½ pound feta cheese
Freshly ground black pepper (about ½ teaspoon)
2 tablespoons vegetable oil
2 tablespoons white vinegar
3 stalks celery
10 pecans or walnuts
½ teaspoon salt

Cut cheese in thin slices; arrange in shallow bowl. Sprinkle generously with pepper. Drizzle 1 tablespoon each oil and vinegar over cheese.

Clean celery stalks; cut into thin slices. Arrange on cheese. Sprinkle with nuts. Drizzle with remaining oil and vinegar; sprinkle with salt. Cover; refrigerate at least 1 hour. Mix well; correct seasoning if necessary.

feta-cheese salad

health salad

Yield: 4 to 6 servings

> 1 head Boston lettuce
> 1 small cucumber
> 2 small tomatoes
> 1 green pepper
> ½ avocado
> 5 radishes
> 1 peach
> 1 slice pineapple (from can)
> 4 ounces mandarin oranges (from can)
> ¼ pound fresh strawberries

Wash lettuce; tear leaves into bite-size pieces.
Cut unpeeled cucumber into thin slices.
Peel tomatoes; cut into slices.
Core, seed, and slice green pepper.
Peel and slice avocado.
Clean and slice radishes.
Peel peach; cube peach and pineapple slice.
Drain oranges.
Hull strawberries; cut in half.
Arrange all ingredients in large bowl.

salad dressing

> 1 small onion, minced
> 2 teaspoons prepared mustard
> 6 tablespoons lemon juice
> ¼ teaspoon salt
> ⅛ teaspoon white pepper
> 3 tablespoons vegetable oil
> 1 sprig parsley, chopped
> 2 teaspoons fresh dill (or ½ teaspoon dried dill)
> ¼ teaspoon dried tarragon
> ¼ teaspoon dried basil

Blend onion thoroughly with mustard, lemon juice, salt, pepper, and oil. Add herbs; correct seasoning if necessary.

Pour dressing over salad; mix gently but thoroughly. Cover salad; marinate about 10 minutes.

Serve salad in a bowl or on a platter.

health salad

fruit salad with nuts

Yield: 4 to 6 servings

1 small honeydew melon
2 oranges
1 cup blue grapes

Lettuce leaves
12 walnut halves

Scoop out melon with melon-baller.
Cut peel from oranges. Remove white membrane; slice crosswise.
Cut grapes in half; remove seeds.
Line glass bowl with lettuce leaves. Arrange melon balls, orange slices, grapes, and walnuts in layers on top of lettuce.

salad dressing

1 8-ounce container yogurt
1 tablespoon lemon juice
1 tablespoon orange juice
1 tablespoon tomato catsup

2 tablespoons evaporated milk
Dash of salt
Dash of white pepper

Mix and blend well all dressing ingredients. Adjust seasonings.
Pour dressing over fruit. Let salad ingredients marinate 30 minutes. Toss salad just before serving.

fruit salad with nuts

garden pea salad

Yield: 4 servings

1 10-ounce package frozen peas	1 cup alfalfa sprouts
½ cup water	½ cup cubed cheddar cheese
¼ cup vegetable oil	¼ cup chopped celery
2½ tablespoons vinegar	¼ cup coarsely chopped
¾ teaspoon salt	cashew nuts (unsalted)
⅛ teaspoon pepper	2 tablespoons plain yogurt
¼ teaspoon thyme	1 tablespoon mayonnaise

Place peas in saucepan with water; cover. Bring to boiling. Remove pan from heat. Let stand 1 or 2 minutes, just until peas are thoroughly heated; drain.

Combine oil, vinegar, salt, pepper, and thyme. Pour over peas. Cover; refrigerate several hours.

Just before serving, remove peas from marinade with slotted spoon. Stir in remaining ingredients.

spinach salad

Yield: 4 servings

salad dressing

2 tablespoons vegetable oil
Juice of 1 lemon
1 tablespoon Dijon-style mustard
1 tablespoon grated Parmesan cheese
1 teaspoon sugar
1 teaspoon Worcestershire sauce
½ teaspoon salt
Dash of pepper

Combine ingredients in small jar with lid. Shake well; chill.

1 bunch or 1 package (10-ounce) fresh spinach
¼ pound fresh mushrooms, sliced
1 hard-cooked egg white, sieved or chopped
¼ cup sunflower seeds

Thoroughly wash spinach; tear into bite-size pieces. Chill in tight plastic bag to crisp.

Combine spinach and mushrooms in large bowl. Toss mixture with dressing. Garnish with egg white and sunflower seeds.

marinated cherry-tomato salad

Yield: 2 to 4 servings

¼ cup vegetable oil
3 tablespoons cider vinegar
½ teaspoon tarragon
½ teaspoon basil
2 tablespoons chopped fresh parsley
¼ teaspoon salt
1¼ teaspoons sugar
Freshly ground pepper to taste
1 cup cherry tomatoes
1 cup sliced mushrooms (¼ pound)

Combine all but tomatoes and mushrooms in small mixing bowl.

Wash tomatoes; remove stems. Cut in halves. Add tomatoes and mushrooms to dressing in bowl.

Stir gently to coat with dressing. Cover; chill 3 to 4 hours, stirring occasionally during marinating period.

To serve, remove tomatoes and mushrooms from dressing; place on bed of lettuce.

Note: If this salad is made in bowl with leakproof cover, bowl can be turned upside down several times while marinating; mushrooms will be bruised less than if stirred.

cheese-stuffed tomatoes

Yield: 4 servings

4 medium tomatoes
2 ounces blue cheese
2 ounces cottage cheese
2 tablespoons evaporated milk
1 stalk celery
¼ teaspoon salt
¼ teaspoon paprika
½ teaspoon chopped chives
4 lettuce leaves

cheese-stuffed tomatoes

Wash tomatoes. Slice off tops; scoop out seeds.

Crumble blue cheese with fork; blend with cottage cheese and milk.

Mince celery; add to cheese. Season with salt and paprika.

Fill tomatoes with cheese mixture. Sprinkle chopped chives over tops. Place tomato tops back on.

Serve tomatoes on lettuce leaves.

marinated yam and broccoli salad

Yield: 4 to 5 servings

 2 cups small fresh broccoli florets
 1½ cups peeled and diced raw yams or sweet potatoes

marinade

 2 tablespoons cider vinegar
 1½ teaspoons vegetable oil
 1½ teaspoons minced fresh onion
 ¼ teaspoon basil
 ¾ teaspoon salt
 ⅛ teaspoon pepper
 1 8-ounce can crushed pineapple in its own juice

Combine broccoli and yams.

In small bowl add vinegar, oil, onion, basil, salt, and pepper to crushed pineapple; stir together. Pour pineapple mixture over broccoli and yams; carefully stir to coat vegetables. Refrigerate overnight, stirring occasionally.

vegetable layered salad

Yield 4 to 6 servings

 1 10-ounce package frozen baby lima beans
 2 cups fresh cauliflower florets, cut into bite-size pieces
 1 small red onion, thinly sliced
 1 cup alfalfa sprouts
 1 cup fresh broccoli florets, cut into bite-size pieces
 1 cup grated cheddar cheese
 ½ cup chopped walnuts
 Italian Salad Dressing (see Index)

Cook lima beans in boiling salted water 5 minutes; drain.

Place layers of cauliflower, lima beans, onion, sprouts, and broccoli in glass salad bowl. Repeat once. Top with cheese and nuts. Cover bowl; chill.

When ready to serve, toss lightly. Pass Italian Salad Dressing.

sunset jellied salad

Here is a colorful golden-orange and red molded salad without the use of artificial colors.

Yield: 8 servings

golden-orange layer

1 envelope unflavored gelatin
4 tablespoons sugar
1 cup orange juice
1 can (11 ounces) mandarin oranges
1 stalk celery, chopped
¾ cup cottage cheese
½ cup plain yogurt

red layer

2 tablespoons sugar
1 envelope unflavored gelatin
1 cup cranberry-juice cocktail
1 10-ounce package frozen strawberries in syrup, thawed
½ cup plain yogurt

Prepare golden-orange layer. Thoroughly stir together gelatin and sugar. Add to orange juice in small saucepan; heat, stirring, over low heat until gelatin has dissolved.

Drain mandarin oranges; reserve syrup. Add water to orange syrup to make ½ cup liquid, if needed. Add reserved syrup to orange juice–gelatin mixture. Chill until partially set. Add orange segments, celery, cottage cheese, and yogurt. Pour into 7-cup salad mold. Chill until set but not firm.

Prepare red layer. Stir together sugar and gelatin. Add to cranberry juice; heat slowly, stirring, until gelatin has dissolved. Add cold strawberries in syrup; stir in yogurt. Pour over golden-orange layer. Chill until firm.

For variation, try substituting one 10-ounce package frozen raspberries in place of strawberries.

jellied vegetable salad

Yield: 4 servings

> 1 package gelatin
> ¼ cup cold water
> 1 cup boiling water
> ¼ cup sugar
> ¼ cup white vinegar
> 2 tablespoons lemon juice
> ½ teaspoon salt
> 1 large cucumber
> ⅓ cup chopped cabbage, red or green
> 2 drops Tabasco
> 2 tablespoons chopped onion
> ½ cup chopped celery
> 2 tablespoons chopped green pepper

Soak gelatin in cold water 3 minutes. Add hot water; stir until dissolved. Add sugar, vinegar, lemon juice, and salt.

Peel cucumber; cut in half lengthwise. Remove seeds; chop.

Combine all ingredients; chill in ring mold 3 hours or more.

molded cranberry salad

Yield: 4 to 6 servings

> 1 envelope unflavored gelatin (1 tablespoon)
> 2 tablespoons sugar
> ½ cup cranberry-juice cocktail
> 2 tablespoons fresh lemon juice
> 1 8-ounce can (1 cup) crushed pineapple, including juice
> 1 16-ounce can whole cranberry sauce
> ½ cup chopped celery
> ½ cup chopped walnuts
> Dash of salt
> 1 cup sour cream

Stir together gelatin and sugar. Add cranberry juice; let gelatin soften. Heat over low heat just until gelatin dissolves. Stir in remaining ingredients. Pour into 5-cup salad mold. Chill until set.

Serve salad on bed of lettuce or other greens.

fruit mold

This molded version of the popular "5-cup" salad doesn't waste the fruit juices.

Yield: 4 to 6 servings

    1 11-ounce can mandarin orange segments, drained; reserve juice
    1 8-ounce can crushed pineapple, drained; reserve juice
    1 cup diced ripe banana
    1 cup shredded coconut
    1 envelope unflavored gelatin
    1 tablespoon sugar
    1 cup plain yogurt
    1 tablespoon mayonnaise
    ½ cup chopped walnuts

Combine orange segments, pineapple, banana, and coconut.

Stir together gelatin and sugar in small saucepan. Add juices from oranges and pineapple. Let set until gelatin has softened. Stir over low heat until gelatin dissolves. Remove from heat. Blend in yogurt and mayonnaise with wire whip until smooth. Add gelatin mixture to fruits. Stir in nuts. Pour into 5-cup mold. Chill overnight or until set.

molded garden pea salad

Yield: 4 to 6 servings

    1 envelope unflavored gelatin
    2 tablespoons sugar
    ¾ cup water
    ¼ cup fresh lemon juice
    ¼ teaspoon salt
    ¾ cup salad dressing
    1¼ cups cream-style cottage cheese
    1½ cups cooked peas
    ½ cup finely chopped green pepper
    1 cup radish sprouts
    1 tablespoon minced fresh onion

Stir together gelatin and sugar. Soften in water. Heat over low heat until gelatin dissolves. Add gelatin mixture to lemon juice, salt, salad dressing, and cottage cheese. Beat until dressing is smooth. Chill until thick and syrupy. Fold in remaining ingredients. Pour into 5-cup mold. Chill until set.

anchovy cheese salad dressing

Yield: 2¼ cups

    2 cups cottage cheese
    1 tablespoon lemon juice
    ¼ cup milk
    ½ teaspoon salt
    6 anchovy fillets
    1 teaspoon paprika
    ¼ teaspoon dry mustard

Place all ingredients in electric blender; blend until creamy. Additional milk may be used if thinner dressing is desired.

italian salad dressing

Yield: 1¼ cups

    1 cup vegetable oil
    ¼ cup vinegar
    1 teaspoon salt
    ½ teaspoon sugar
    1 teaspoon minced onion
    ½ teaspoon parsley flakes
    ¼ teaspoon oregano
    ¼ teaspoon dry mustard
    ⅛ teaspoon pepper
    Dash of cayenne
    1 garlic clove, minced

Combine ingredients in jar; cover. Shake vigorously; chill. Shake again before serving.

tangy yogurt salad dressing

Yield: 1¼ cups

    1 cup yogurt
    3 tablespoons lemon juice
    ½ teaspoon dry mustard
    1 minced clove garlic
    ½ teaspoon onion salt
    1 teaspoon paprika

Combine ingredients; chill. Serve on green salads for nutritious low-calorie dressing.

yogurt–blue-cheese salad dressing

Yield: 2 cups

> 4 ounces blue cheese, crumbled
> 1 cup mayonnaise
> 2 teaspoons fresh lemon juice
> 1 tablespoon grated onion
> ½ cup plain yogurt
> Dash of white pepper

Combine cheese, mayonnaise, lemon juice, and onion. Fold in yogurt and pepper; chill.

very low-calorie salad dressing

Yield: ½ cup

> ½ cup wine vinegar
> ½ clove garlic, crushed
> ¼ teaspoon tarragon
> 1 tablespoon chopped parsley
> ¼ teaspoon oregano
> ¼ teaspoon salt

Shake ingredients well; pour over salad. Can be stored in refrigerator several weeks.

breads and granolas

apricot bran loaf

Yield: 9 × 5-inch loaf

1 cup dried fruit (apricots, pears,
    prunes, or apples)
Boiling water
2 tablespoons sugar
1½ cups sifted all-purpose flour
½ cup sugar

4 teaspoons baking powder
½ teaspoon salt
1½ cups whole-bran cereal
1 cup milk
2 eggs, slightly beaten
⅓ cup vegetable oil

Cut dried fruit into small pieces with scissors. Pour boiling water over fruit to cover. Soak 10 minutes; drain well. Stir 2 tablespoons sugar into fruit.

Sift together flour, ½ cup sugar, baking powder, and salt.

Mix together cereal, milk, eggs, and oil. Add cereal–egg mixture to flour mixture; stir until moistened. Stir in fruit. Pour into greased 9 × 5-inch bread pan. Bake in preheated 350°F oven 1 hour. Remove from pan; cool on rack.

bran whole-wheat bread

Yield: Two 9 × 5-inch loaves

1 cup water
¾ cup milk
¾ cup coarse bran
½ cup molasses
1 tablespoon salt

6 tablespoons butter or margarine
½ cup very warm water
2 packages active dry yeast
3 cups whole-wheat flour (unsifted)
3 cups white all-purpose flour (unsifted)

Heat 1 cup water and milk to boiling point. Stir in bran, molasses, salt, and butter. Cook to lukewarm if necessary.

Put warm water and yeast into large warm bowl; stir until dissolved. Add bran mixture and whole-wheat flour; beat until smooth. Add enough white flour to make dough stiff enough to knead. Knead on floured board 8 to 10 minutes or until smooth and elastic. Place in greased bowl; turn once to grease top. Cover; let rise until double (about 45 minutes).

Punch down dough; shape into 2 loaves. Place in 2 greased 9 × 5-inch loaf pans; cover. Let rise until dough reaches tops of pans.

Bake in preheated 375° oven 45 minutes or until done. Remove from pans; cool on racks.

raisin and bran bread

Yield: Three 8½ × 4½-inch loaves

2 cups all-purpose flour
1 cup whole-wheat flour
1 tablespoon toasted wheat germ
2 packages active dry yeast
1 cup rolled oats (regular or quick-cooking)
1 cup whole-bran cereal
1 cup seedless raisins

1½ cups cottage cheese
2 tablespoons vegetable oil
1 tablespoon salt
½ cup honey
2½ cups boiling water
About 4½ cups additional
   all-purpose flour

Stir together 2 cups all-purpose flour, whole-wheat flour, wheat germ, and yeast in large mixing bowl. Set aside.

Combine oats, cereal, raisins, cottage cheese, oil, salt, and honey in separate bowl. Cover with boiling water; stir until thoroughly mixed. Cool to lukewarm.

Add cottage-cheese mixture to dry ingredients in mixer bowl. Beat ½ minute at lowest speed of electric mixer, scraping bowl constantly. Beat 3 minutes at highest speed. Stir in about 4½ cups flour by hand, until mixture forms moderately stiff dough. Knead on floured board until smooth and elastic, about 10 minutes. Place in greased bowl, turning once to grease surface. Cover with dampened towel; let rise until double in bulk, about 1 hour.

Punch down dough; divide into thirds. Cover; let rest 10 minutes. Shape into 3 loaves. Place in 3 greased 8½ × 4½ × 2½-inch loaf pans. Brush tops lightly with vegetable oil; cover. Let rise until double, about 35 to 45 minutes.

Bake in 375°F oven 35 to 40 minutes or until golden brown. Remove from pans; let cool on rack.

new england harvest bread

Yield: 2 loaves

⅔ cup shortening
1 cup packed brown sugar
1¼ cups sugar
4 eggs, beaten
1 15-ounce can winter squash or 2 cups
   unseasoned cooked winter (butternut,
   acorn, or harvard) squash
⅔ cup water
1¼ cups all-purpose flour

2 cups whole-wheat pastry flour
¾ teaspoon baking powder
2 teaspoons baking soda
1½ teaspoons salt
1 teaspoon cinnamon
½ teaspoon ground cloves
1 cup chopped walnuts
1 cup chopped dates

Cream together shortening and sugars in large mixing bowl. Add eggs; beat well. Stir in squash and water.

Sift together flours, baking powder, soda, salt, cinnamon, and cloves. Add to squash mixture; stir until blended. Stir in nuts and dates. Pour into 2 well-greased 8½ × 4½-inch bread pans. Bake at 350°F 65 to 75 minutes, until toothpick inserted in center comes out clean.

date nut bread

Yield: 1 loaf (9 × 5 inches)

    1 cup boiling water
    1 8-ounce package pitted dates, chopped
    ¼ cup shortening
    ½ cup all-purpose flour
    1 cup whole-wheat flour
    ¼ cup wheat germ
    ½ cup sugar
    1 teaspoon baking soda
    ¼ teaspoon salt
    1 egg, slightly beaten
    ¾ cup sliced almonds

Pour boiling water over dates. Add shortening; let stand.

Meanwhile combine flours, wheat germ, sugar, soda, and salt. Stir in date mixture, egg, and ½ cup almonds; mix well. Spoon batter into greased loaf pan. Sprinkle reserved nuts on top. Bake at 350°F 50 minutes or until done. Test for doneness with cake-tester or toothpick. Remove from pan; cool on rack.

date nut bread

molasses brown bread

Yield: 9 × 5-inch loaf

2½ cups whole-wheat flour
1½ cups wheat germ
⅓ cup brown sugar
½ teaspoon salt
1 cup raisins (mixed, light and dark)
2 teaspoons baking soda
1⅞ cups buttermilk
⅓ cup molasses

Preheat oven to 325°F.
Grease 9 × 5 × 3-inch pan.
Combine flour, wheat germ, brown sugar, salt, and raisins in mixing bowl; mix well.

In second mixing bowl mix soda, buttermilk, and molasses, using wooden spoon. Mixture will start to bubble; immediately stir into dry ingredients. Spoon batter into greased pan; bake at once. Bread is done when toothpick comes out clean, about 1 hour. Turn out of pan; cool on wire rack.

orange nut bread

Yield: 9 × 5-inch loaf

2 cups sifted all-purpose flour
¾ cup sifted whole-wheat flour
⅓ cup wheat germ
½ cup sugar
1 tablespoon baking powder
½ teaspoon baking soda
1 cup orange juice
⅓ cup vegetable oil
1 egg, beaten
⅓ cup walnuts, chopped
2 tablespoons grated orange rind

Measure dry ingredients; sift together into large bowl. Stir in remaining ingredients until blended well. Pour batter into greased 9 × 5-inch bread pan. Bake 55 to 60 minutes in preheated 350°F oven. Check center with cake-tester or toothpick. Immediately remove bread from pan.

pumpkin bread

Yield: Two 9 × 5-inch loaves

⅔ cup shortening
2½ cups sugar
4 eggs
2 cups cooked pumpkin
⅔ cup water
1 cup all-purpose flour
2 cups whole-wheat flour
2 teaspoons baking soda
1½ teaspoons salt
½ teaspoon baking powder
1 teaspoon ground cloves
1 teaspoon ground cinnamon
⅔ cup chopped nuts
1 cup raisins

Cream shortening and sugar in large bowl. Blend in eggs, pumpkin, and water.

Combine remaining ingredients, except nuts and raisins, in separate bowl. Add to pumpkin mixture; mix well. Stir in nuts and raisins. Pour into 2 greased 9 × 5-inch loaf pans. Bake at 350°F 60 to 70 minutes or until done.

rye bread

rye bread

Yield: 2 round loaves

2 packages dry yeast
½ cup warm water
1½ cups lukewarm milk
2 tablespoons sugar
1 teaspoon salt
½ cup molasses
2 tablespoons butter or margarine
2 tablespoons caraway seeds (optional)
3¼ cups unsifted rye flour
2½ cups unsifted all-purpose flour

Dissolve yeast in warm water.

Combine milk, sugar, and salt in large bowl. Use mixer to beat in molasses, butter, yeast mixture, caraway seeds if desired, and 1 cup rye flour. Use wooden spoon to mix in remaining rye flour. Add white flour by stirring until dough is stiff enough to knead. Knead 5 to 10 minutes, adding flour as needed. If dough sticks to hands and board, add more flour. Cover dough; let rise 1 to 1½ hours or until double.

Punch down dough; divide to form 2 round loaves. Let loaves rise on greased baking sheet until double, about 1½ hours.

Preheat oven to 375°F. Bake bread 30 to 35 minutes.

triticale french bread

Yield: 2 loaves

  2 cups lukewarm water
  2 tablespoons or 2 packages dry yeast
  1½ tablespoons honey
  1 tablespoon salt
  2 tablespoons vegetable oil
  2½ cups all-purpose flour
  1 cup whole-wheat flour
  ¾ cup triticale flour
  Additional flour for kneading

Combine water, yeast, and honey in large mixing bowl. Let stand 5 minutes. Stir in salt and oil. Add 1 cup all-purpose flour and whole-wheat flour. Beat on low speed of electric mixer until blended, then beat at medium speed 3 minutes. Stir in triticale flour and additional 1½ cups all-purpose flour by hand. Turn out onto well-floured surface; cover loosely with plastic wrap. Let rest 10 to 15 minutes.

Knead dough 10 to 12 minutes, working in additional all-purpose flour as required. Place dough in greased bowl, turning once to grease top. Cover with damp towel; let rise 1 hour.

Punch down dough; let rest 10 minutes.

To shape into loaves, divide dough in half. Roll each half into rectangle length of long baking pan or cookie sheet. Roll tightly as for jelly roll, pinching seams and ends together. Place seam-side-down on baking sheet sprinkled with cornmeal. Cover with towel; let rise 20 minutes.

While dough is rising, preheat oven to 425°F. Place shallow pan half-filled with water on lower rack. Just before placing bread in oven, spray quickly with water (a plant mister works well), or brush with pastry brush. Bake at 425°F 10 minutes. During this period, quickly open oven door and "mist" bread at least 3 times. Reduce oven temperature to 350°F; bake 30 minutes. Place bread on rack to cool.

maple–bran triticale bread

Yield: 2 loaves

1 tablespoon or package active dry yeast
3 cups lukewarm water
⅓ cup pure maple syrup
1 cup nonfat dry milk powder
4 cups all-purpose flour
4 teaspoons salt
⅓ cup vegetable oil

⅓ cup bran
¼ cup wheat germ
1½ cups triticale flour
2 to 2½ cups all-purpose flour
Additional all-purpose
   flour for kneading
Melted butter

Dissolve yeast in warm water in large mixing bowl. Stir in maple syrup, dry milk, and 4 cups all-purpose flour. Beat vigorously with spoon, about 100 strokes. Cover with damp towel; let rise about 1 hour.

Stir in salt and oil. Add bran, wheat germ, and triticale flour; beat well. Blend in all-purpose flour until mixture pulls away from sides of bowl. Knead on floured surface 10 minutes. Place in greased bowl, turning once to grease top of dough. Cover with damp towel; let rise until double in bulk, about 1 hour.

Punch down dough. Let rest 30 minutes. Shape into 2 loaves. Place in 2 9½ × 5½-inch greased bread pans. Brush tops with melted butter. Let rise until almost double, about 35 to 45 minutes.

Bake at 400°F 10 minutes, then at 350°F about 40 minutes or until done. Remove from pans to cool.

triticale whole-wheat bread

Yield: 2 loaves

2 tablespoons active dry yeast (2 packages)
3 cups lukewarm water
⅓ cup honey
1 cup nonfat dry milk powder
2 cups all-purpose flour
2 cups whole-wheat flour
4 teaspoons salt

⅓ cup vegetable oil
1 cup triticale flour
2½ to 3 cups additional
   whole-wheat flour
All-purpose flour for kneading
Melted butter

Dissolve yeast in water in large mixing bowl. Stir in honey, dry milk, all-purpose flour, and 2 cups whole-wheat flour. Beat vigorously, about 100 strokes. Cover with damp towel; let rise 50 minutes.

Stir in salt and oil. Add triticale and whole-wheat flours. Knead on floured surface 10 minutes. Place in greased bowl, turning once to grease top of dough. Cover with damp towel; let rise until double in bulk, about 1 hour.

Punch dough down. Let rest 30 minutes. Shape into 2 loaves. Place in 2 9½ × 5½-inch greased bread pans. Brush with melted butter. Let rise until almost double, 30 to 40 minutes.

Bake at 400°F 10 minutes, then at 350°F 40 to 50 minutes or until done. Remove from pans to cool.

cinnamon apricot–prune ring

Freshly baked and warm from the oven, this is one of the great joys of bread-making!

Yield: 1 large coffee cake

dough

1½ to 1¾ cups all-purpose flour
1 tablespoon or 1 package active dry yeast
⅓ cup nonfat dry milk powder
¼ cup honey
¼ cup butter or margarine
1 teaspoon salt
¾ cup boiling water
1 egg, beaten
½ teaspoon grated lemon peel
1 cup whole-wheat flour
2 tablespoons wheat germ
Flour for kneading
2 tablespoons butter or margarine, melted

Stir together 1 cup all-purpose flour, yeast, and milk powder in large mixer bowl.

Combine honey, butter, and salt in another small bowl. Pour boiling water over; stir until butter melts. Let cool until comfortably warm (115 to 120°F). Add to flour mixture along with egg and lemon peel. Beat at low speed of electric mixer to blend ingredients, scraping bowl as needed, then beat at high speed 3 minutes. Stir in whole-wheat flour and wheat germ by hand. Add remaining ½ to ¾ cup flour. Knead on floured surface until smooth, 5 to 7 minutes. Place in greased bowl, turning once to grease dough. Cover with damp towel; let rise until double (1½ to 2 hours).

Punch down dough; turn onto floured surface. Let rest 10 minutes. Roll to 18 × 12-inch rectangle. Brush with 1½ tablespoons melted butter. Spread with filling. Starting with long side, roll as for jelly roll. Carefully transfer to greased cookie sheet. Form into circle, placing sealed edge down. Using sharp scissors, make cuts ¾ of way through ring at 1-inch intervals. Turn 1 piece to center, next to outside; repeat around ring. Brush with remaining ½ tablespoon melted butter. Cover lightly; let rise in warm place until nearly double in size, about 1 hour.

Bake in preheated oven at 375°F 20 to 25 minutes. Drizzle with Confectioners' Sugar Icing while warm, or, if more decorative effect is desired, wait until ring cools, then spread with icing.

apricot–prune filling

1 cup diced dried apricots
1 cup diced dried prunes
1½ cups water
3 tablespoons sugar
1 teaspoon cinnamon
Dash of ground cloves

Combine apricots, prunes, and water in saucepan. Cook and stir over low heat until thickened, about 15 minutes.

Combine sugar, cinnamon, and cloves. Stir into apricot–prune mixture. Let cool.

confectioners' sugar icing

1 cup sifted confectioners' sugar
¼ teaspoon almond extract
About 1½ tablespoons milk

Beat ingredients together until smooth.

club rolls

Yield: 14 to 16 rolls

2 packages dry yeast
¼ cup warm water
¼ cup butter or margarine
1¾ cups skim milk, scalded,
    cooled to lukewarm
1 teaspoon salt
¼ cup honey
2 cups stone-ground
    whole-wheat or
    cracked-wheat flour
3 to 4 cups all-purpose flour

club rolls

Dissolve yeast in warm water.

Combine butter, milk, salt, and honey; stir into yeast. Add whole-wheat flour; stir until well mixed. Add 2 cups all-purpose flour; mix until smooth. Gradually add more flour until dough can be handled without sticking to fingers. Knead on lightly floured board 10 minutes or until smooth and elastic. Add remaining flour as needed. Place dough in greased bowl, turning once to grease surface. Cover; let rise until double in bulk (about 1½ hours).

Punch down dough; cover. Let rest 10 minutes. Shape into 14 to 16 oblong rolls; place on greased baking sheets. Cover; let rise until almost double (about 45 minutes).

Bake in preheated 400°F oven about 15 minutes or until browned.

corn bread with yogurt

Yield: 9 × 9-inch pan

2 eggs, beaten
3 tablespoons honey
¼ cup butter or margarine, melted
1 cup plain yogurt
1 cup whole-wheat pastry flour

⅔ cup cornmeal
2 teaspoons baking powder
½ teaspoon baking soda
½ teaspoon salt

Beat together eggs and honey. Blend in butter. Add yogurt; stir until smooth.
Stir together flour, cornmeal, baking powder, soda, and salt until well mixed. Add to yogurt mixture; stir just until thoroughly moistened. Pour into greased 9 × 9-inch pan. Bake at 400°F 25 to 30 minutes.
Cut bread into squares. Serve warm with butter.

nutty carrot muffins

These nutritious muffins are simplified with the aid of an electric blender.

Yield: 12 muffins

1 cup whole-wheat pastry flour
¾ cup all-purpose flour
1 teaspoon salt
2½ teaspoons baking powder
¼ cup brown sugar
¼ cup nonfat dry milk powder

⅔ cup water
⅓ cup vegetable oil
1 egg
1 large carrot, cut into ½-inch slices
½ cup unsalted peanuts

Combine flours, salt, baking powder, sugar, and milk powder. Stir until thoroughly mixed; set aside.
Place remaining ingredients in blender. Blend until smooth. Pour wet ingredients over flour mixture. Stir until flour is moistened. Pour into 12 greased muffin cups. Bake at 400°F 25 minutes or until done.

prune-nugget muffins

Yield: 1 dozen

½ cup all-purpose flour
½ cup whole-wheat pastry flour
¼ cup wheat germ
2 teaspoons baking powder
½ teaspoon salt
1 teaspoon grated lemon rind
1 egg, beaten

¼ cup honey
⅔ cup milk
¼ cup vegetable oil
1 cup prune "nuggets" (cut pitted
  prunes into 4 to 6 pieces each,
  using kitchen scissors)
⅓ cup chopped walnuts or pecans

Stir together flours, wheat germ, baking powder, salt, and lemon rind in mixing bowl.
Combine egg, honey, milk, and oil in separate bowl. Pour wet ingredients over dry ingredients; stir just until blended. Gently stir in prunes and nuts. Pour into 12 well-greased muffin-pan cups. Bake at 400°F about 18 minutes.

maple cottage-cheese rolls

Yield: About 3 dozen

2 packages active dry yeast
1 cup very warm water
½ cup maple syrup
¼ cup nonfat dry milk powder
½ cup rolled oats
1 cup creamed cottage cheese
1 cup all-purpose flour

2 tablespoons vegetable oil
2½ teaspoons salt
½ teaspoon baking soda
1 egg, beaten
About 2½ cups whole-wheat flour
Additional flour for kneading

Dissolve yeast in water.

Combine maple syrup, milk powder, oats, and cottage cheese in large mixing bowl. Add dissolved yeast. Stir in all-purpose flour; beat with spoon about 100 strokes. Partially cover bowl; let rise 50 to 60 minutes.

Stir in oil, salt, soda, and egg. Gradually add about 2½ cups whole-wheat flour, stirring well, until dough is moderately stiff. Knead on floured surface until smooth, 8 to 10 minutes. Cover loosely with plastic wrap, then a clean towel. Let rest 10 to 15 minutes.

Punch down dough. Shape into rolls. Place in greased pans; cover loosely with towel. Let rise until double.

Bake in 375°F oven 12 to 15 minutes.

whole-wheat refrigerator rolls

Yield: 2½ dozen

½ cup lukewarm water
1 tablespoon or package dry yeast
⅓ cup honey
2 eggs
⅓ cup vegetable oil
1 cup warm water
1¼ teaspoons salt
2½ cups whole-wheat flour
1½ cups all-purpose flour

Pour ½ cup lukewarm water into large mixer bowl. Sprinkle with yeast. Let stand 5 minutes. Add honey, eggs, oil, water, and salt. Beat on low speed of electric mixer 2 minutes. Add whole-wheat flour. Beat at low speed to blend, then on medium-high 3 to 4 minutes. Stir in all-purpose flour by hand. Cover tightly with plastic wrap. Refrigerate 1 to 6 days.

To bake, drop spoonfuls of dough into greased muffin pans, filling each about ½ full. Press each flat with fingers. Let rise 2½ to 3 hours.

Bake at 400°F about 10 minutes or until done.

granola

Yield: 12 cups

6 cups rolled oats
2 cups wheat flakes (or rolled oats)
1 cup chopped cashew nuts
1 cup unsweetened flaked coconut
1 cup wheat germ
½ cup instant dry milk powder
3 tablespoons flax seeds (optional)
2 tablespoons brewer's yeast
½ cup vegetable oil, preferably safflower
½ cup honey
1 tablespoon vanilla

Combine rolled oats and wheat flakes in Dutch oven. Heat, uncovered, in 400°F oven about 45 minutes, until browned. Watch carefully; stir often, especially during last half of browning period.

Remove from oven. Stir in nuts, coconut, wheat germ, milk powder, flax seeds, and yeast. Bake 5 minutes. Remove from oven.

Combine oil, honey, and vanilla; pour over granola. Stir well; place in oven 5 minutes. Remove; let cool thoroughly. Store in airtight container.

fruited almond granola

Yield: 11 cups

5 cups rolled oats
¾ cup orange juice
½ cup wheat germ
2 tablespoons nonfat dry milk powder
¼ teaspoon salt
3 tablespoons vegetable oil
3 tablespoons honey
¼ teaspoon almond extract
1 cup chopped dates
½ cup diced dried apricots
½ cup diced pitted prunes
¾ cup coarsely chopped almonds
1½ cups grapenuts cereal

In Dutch oven or large ovenproof casserole dish stir together oats and orange juice until evenly mixed. Bake in 350°F oven until oats are dry and browned, about 40 to 50 minutes. Stir often, especially during last half of browning time.

Combine wheat germ, milk powder, and salt. Stir into oats.

In small pan or metal measuring cup, heat together oil and honey until warm. Add almond extract. Pour over oat mixture; stir until well combined. Place oat mixture back in oven; toast 5 to 7 minutes, stirring if necessary. Stir in remaining ingredients. Cool thoroughly, then store in airtight container.

cookies

apricot balls

Yield: 20 to 24 balls

> 1 cup dried apricots
> ½ cup walnuts
> ½ cup coconut
> 2 tablespoons wheat germ
> 4 tablespoons orange juice
> ⅓ cup finely chopped walnuts

Put apricots, ½ cup walnuts, and coconut through food grinder. Add wheat germ and orange juice; mix well. Form into 1-inch balls. Roll in chopped walnuts. Refrigerate.

cheese crisps

Yield: 4 dozen

> ½ pound cheddar cheese, grated (2 cups)
> ⅓ cup grated Parmesan cheese
> ½ cup butter or margarine, room temperature
> ¼ cup water
> ¾ cup whole-wheat pastry flour
> ⅓ cup all-purpose flour
> 1 tablespoon toasted wheat germ
> ¼ teaspoon salt
> Dash of cayenne (optional)
> 1 cup rolled oats
> ⅛ teaspoon paprika

Thoroughly blend cheeses, butter, and water. Add flours, wheat germ, salt, and cayenne; mix well. Stir in rolled oats. Divide dough in half. Form into 2 rolls, each about 1½ inches in diameter (about 6 inches long). Wrap tightly; refrigerate until well chilled, about 4 hours, or up to 1 week.

Slice ⅛ to ¼ inch thick; sprinkle with paprika. Bake on greased baking sheet at 400°F 8 to 10 minutes. Cool on rack.

If less uniform shape is desired, dough can be shaped into small (1¼-inch) balls immediately after mixing and flattened with hands onto baking sheet. Sprinkle with paprika; bake in 400°F oven 8 to 10 minutes, until golden brown.

chocolate nut cookies

Yield: 3 dozen

- ½ cup butter or margarine, softened
- ½ cup brown sugar
- ¼ cup honey
- 1 teaspoon vanilla
- 1 egg, beaten
- 2 1-ounce squares unsweetened chocolate, melted
- ¾ cup whole-wheat pastry flour
- 2 tablespoons nonfat dry milk powder
- ½ teaspoon salt
- ⅛ teaspoon baking soda
- ¾ cup chopped peanuts (unsalted)
- 1 cup sunflower seeds (unsalted)

Cream together butter, sugar, and honey. Blend in vanilla, egg, and chocolate.

Stir together flour, milk powder, salt, and soda. Add to creamed mixture; mix well. Stir in peanuts and sunflower seeds. Drop by teaspoonfuls onto lightly greased baking sheet, about 2 inches apart. Bake at 375°F 8 to 10 minutes. Remove from pan to cool.

date–pumpkin cookies

Yield: 4 dozen

- 1½ cups whole-wheat pastry flour
- 2 teaspoons baking powder
- ½ teaspoon baking soda
- ½ teaspoon salt
- 1 teaspoon cinnamon
- ½ teaspoon nutmeg
- ⅛ teaspoon ground cloves
- ⅔ cup butter or margarine, softened
- ½ cup sugar
- ½ cup packed brown sugar
- 2 eggs, beaten
- 1¼ cups cooked or canned pumpkin
- 1 teaspoon vanilla
- 1 cup chopped dates
- 1 cup rolled oats
- ½ cup chopped nuts

Stir together flour, baking powder, soda, salt, cinnamon, nutmeg, and cloves until well blended.

Cream butter and sugars. Add eggs; beat well. Stir in pumpkin and vanilla.

Blend flour mixture with pumpkin mixture; stir thoroughly. Add dates, oats, and nuts; mix well. Drop by teaspoonfuls onto greased baking sheet. Bake at 375°F about 12 minutes. Remove to rack to cool.

molasses gingersnaps

Yield: 3 to 4 dozen

½ cup shortening
1 cup sugar
1 cup molasses
½ cup water
⅓ cup wheat germ
3 cups all-purpose flour
1½ cups whole-wheat flour

1½ teaspoons salt
1½ teaspoons baking soda
1½ teaspoons ginger
½ teaspoon cloves
½ teaspoon nutmeg
¼ teaspoon allspice

Thoroughly cream shortening and sugar. Blend in molasses and water. Stir in wheat germ.

Sift dry ingredients together; gradually beat into sugar–fat mixture. Cover; chill dough 3 hours or more.

Roll dough ¼ inch thick on lightly floured board; cut into 3-inch circles. Sprinkle lightly with sugar; place on greased baking sheet. Bake at 375°F 10 to 12 minutes. Let cookies cool on baking sheet 3 minutes. Remove; cool on wire rack.

cinnamon graham crackers

Yield: 3 dozen

½ cup butter or margarine
⅔ cup brown sugar
1 teaspoon vanilla
1 cup all-purpose flour
2 cups whole-wheat flour
1 teaspoon baking powder
½ teaspoon baking soda
¼ teaspoon salt
1½ teaspoons cinnamon
½ to ⅔ cup milk

Cream together butter and sugar. Add vanilla; beat well.

Stir together flours, baking powder, soda, salt, and cinnamon until well combined. Add flour mixture alternately with milk to creamed mixture, adding just enough milk that mixture is consistency of pie dough and holds together. Divide dough into thirds. On floured board roll out each portion into ⅛-inch-thick rectangle. Cut into squares (3 × 3 inches); place on greased baking sheets. Prick each square thoroughly with fork. Bake at 350°F 10 to 12 minutes, until edges are crisp and brown.

Suggestion: Let children help make these into "animal" crackers by cutting them out with animal-shaped cookie cutters. Don't forget to prick tops!

honey granola cookies

Yield: 2 to 2½ dozen

> ½ cup vegetable oil
> ½ cup honey
> 2 eggs, beaten
> 1 teaspoon vanilla
> 1¼ cups whole-wheat pastry flour
> ½ teaspoon salt
> ½ teaspoon baking soda
> 1 cup granola

Combine oil and honey. Stir in eggs and vanilla.

Combine flour, salt, and soda. Stir into wet ingredients. Add granola; mix well. Drop by teaspoonfuls onto greased baking sheet. Bake at 325°F 10 to 12 minutes or until done.

lunch-box specials

Yield: 3 dozen

> ¾ cup whole-wheat pastry flour
> 2 tablespoons all-purpose flour
> 2 tablespoons nonfat dry milk powder
> ½ teaspoon baking soda
> ½ teaspoon salt
> ⅔ cup butter or margarine, slightly softened
> ½ cup packed brown sugar
> 1 egg, beaten
> 1 teaspoon vanilla
> 1 cup grated cheddar cheese
> 1¼ cups rolled oats
> ¼ cup toasted wheat germ
> ¼ cup sunflower seeds or finely chopped walnuts
> 1 tablespoon flax seeds (if not available, omit, or substitute sesame seeds)
> 6 slices bacon, cooked crisp, crumbled

Combine flours, milk powder, soda, and salt; set aside.

Cream together butter and sugar until fluffy. Beat in egg and vanilla. Add flour mixture; stir well. Add remaining ingredients; stir until well distributed. Drop by teaspoonfuls onto greased cookie sheet. Bake in 350°F oven 12 to 14 minutes, until lightly browned around edges. Cool briefly on cookie sheet, then remove to rack to cool.

old-fashioned peanut-butter cookies

Yield: 5 to 6 dozen large cookies

 2 cups shortening, room temperature
 2 cups peanut butter, room temperature
 1⅔ cups sugar
 2 cups brown sugar
 5 eggs
 2 teaspoons vanilla
 3 cups all-purpose flour
 2 cups whole-wheat flour
 2 teaspoons baking soda
 1 teaspoon salt

Thoroughly cream shortening and peanut butter. Beat in sugars. Add eggs and vanilla; beat.

Combine dry ingredients; mix well. Blend dry ingredients into peanut-butter mixture. Shape into 1-inch balls. Place 2 inches apart on ungreased cookie sheet. Flatten with fork tines in crisscross pattern or with base of glass. Bake at 375°F 10 minutes.

chewy peanut–oat cookies

Yield: 3 dozen

 ¼ cup butter or margarine, softened
 ¼ cup shortening, softened
 ⅔ cup packed brown sugar
 1 egg, beaten
 ½ cup chunky peanut butter
 1½ teaspoons vanilla
 ½ cup all-purpose flour
 ½ cup whole-wheat pastry flour
 ½ teaspoon baking soda
 ½ teaspoon salt
 1 cup rolled oats
 ½ cup chopped peanuts

Cream together butter, shortening, and sugar. Add egg; beat well. Stir in peanut butter and vanilla; beat smooth.

Combine flours, soda, and salt; stir until well mixed. Stir flour mixture into butter–sugar mixture. Add oats and peanuts. Drop from teaspoon onto greased cookie sheets. Flatten slightly with fork. Bake in 350°F oven 12 to 14 minutes.

sweet-potato cookies

Yield: 3 dozen

⅓ cup butter or margarine
⅓ cup brown sugar
⅓ cup honey
1 egg, beaten
1 cup whole-wheat pastry flour
⅓ cup nonfat dry milk powder
1 teaspoon baking powder
¼ teaspoon baking soda
¾ teaspoon salt
¼ teaspoon cinnamon
¼ teaspoon nutmeg
3 tablespoons wheat germ
1 cup shredded peeled sweet potato
1 teaspoon grated lemon rind
¼ cup grated coconut
1¼ cups rolled oats
⅓ cup chopped nuts

Cream together butter, sugar, and honey. Beat in egg.

Stir together flour, dry milk, baking powder, soda, salt, cinnamon, nutmeg, and wheat germ. Add to egg mixture; beat well. Stir in sweet potato, lemon rind, coconut, oats, and nuts; mix well. Drop by teaspoonfuls onto greased baking sheet. Bake at 375°F 10 to 12 minutes. Cool on rack.

apple–oat bars

Yield: 18 bars

1 cup whole-wheat pastry flour
½ teaspoon baking soda
½ teaspoon salt
1 teaspoon cinnamon
½ cup packed brown sugar
1½ cups rolled oats
½ cup butter or margarine, melted
1 egg, beaten
1½ teaspoons vanilla
⅓ cup chopped walnuts
2 cups thinly sliced peeled apples (3 medium apples)

Stir together flour, soda, salt, and cinnamon until evenly mixed. Add brown sugar and oats. Stir in butter, egg, and vanilla; mix well. Place half of dough in bottom of greased 9-inch-square baking pan. Sprinkle nuts over dough. Arrange apple slices over nuts. Sprinkle remaining dough over apples; press lightly. Bake at 350°F 25 to 30 minutes. Cool; sprinkle with confectioners' sugar, if desired. Cut into bars.

applesauce brownie squares

Yield: 16 squares

½ cup butter or margarine
2 (1-ounce) squares unsweetened chocolate
¾ cup sugar
2 eggs, beaten
¾ cup applesauce
1¼ teaspoons vanilla
1 cup whole-wheat pastry flour
½ teaspoon baking powder
¼ teaspoon baking soda
¼ teaspoon salt

chocolate nut topping

2 tablespoons sugar
¼ cup chopped nuts
½ cup semisweet chocolate pieces

Melt together butter and chocolate in small saucepan over low heat. Add sugar, eggs, applesauce, and vanilla; beat well.

Stir together flour, baking powder, soda, and salt until evenly combined. Add to chocolate mixture; beat well. Pour batter into greased 8-inch-square baking pan.

Combine topping ingredients. Sprinkle over batter. Bake in 350°F oven 30 to 35 minutes, until toothpick inserted in center comes out clean. Cool; cut into squares.

granola squares

Dates and the flavor of oranges make these special!

Yield: 24 squares

1 cup butter or margarine, softened
1½ cups packed brown sugar
¼ cup honey
2 eggs, beaten
¼ cup orange juice
1½ teaspoons grated orange rind
1 teaspoon vanilla
1 cup all-purpose flour
¾ cup whole-wheat pastry flour
½ cup nonfat dry milk powder
1 teaspoon salt
1 teaspoon baking powder
2½ cups granola (homemade or co-op variety)
½ cup chopped dates

Cream butter and sugar. Add honey, eggs, and orange juice; beat well. Stir in orange rind and vanilla.

Stir together flours, dry milk, salt, and baking powder in separate bowl. Add to butter mixture; beat until smooth. Stir in granola and dates. Pour into greased 9 × 12-inch baking pan. Bake at 350°F 40 to 50 minutes or until done. Cool; cut into squares.

mincemeat crumble squares

Yield: 16 squares

> **1 9-ounce package mincemeat**
> **½ cup water**
> **¼ cup chopped walnuts**
> **½ cup butter or margarine, softened**
> **1 cup grated cheddar cheese**
> **½ teaspoon vanilla**
> **1¼ cups plus 2 tablespoons whole-wheat pastry flour**
> **2 tablespoons wheat germ**
> **⅛ teaspoon salt**
> **2 tablespoons sugar**
> **2 tablespoons sunflower seeds**

Crumble mincemeat into small saucepan. Add water; cook, stirring, until slightly thickened, 3 to 4 minutes. Remove from heat. Add walnuts; cool.

Cream butter. Add cheese and vanilla; cream together until thoroughly blended. With pastry blender cut in 1¼ cups whole-wheat pastry flour, wheat germ, and salt. Divide dough in half. Press half in bottom of 8 × 8-inch baking pan. Bake at 400°F 6 to 8 minutes.

Add remaining 2 tablespoons flour, sugar, and sunflower seeds to second half of dough; mix until crumbly.

Spread mincemeat evenly over baked crust. Top with remaining dough. Press lightly with fingers. Bake at 375°F 30 to 35 minutes or until golden brown. Cool; cut into squares.

german spice bars

Yield: 2½ dozen

> **4 eggs, slightly beaten**
> **1 cup sugar**
> **½ cup brown sugar**
> **2 cups whole-wheat flour**
> **½ teaspoon baking soda**
> **1 teaspoon cinnamon**
> **½ teaspoon cloves**
> **¼ teaspoon nutmeg**
> **¼ teaspoon cardamom**
> **⅓ cup candied fruit**
> **⅓ cup chopped almonds**

Beat together eggs and sugars in medium bowl.

Sift together flour, soda, and spices in separate bowl. Gradually beat flour mixture into sugar mixture. Add fruit and nuts; stir to blend. Refrigerate batter 3 hours or more.

With moistened knife, spread tablespoon batter into 1½ × 2½-inch bar (about ¼ inch thick) on well-greased cookie sheet. Let stand overnight at room temperature.

Bake at 350°F 15 minutes.

Cookies are best when served after storing for several days in covered container.

Picture on opposite page: german spice bars

bean bars

Yield: 24 bars

 1 cup whole-wheat pastry flour
 ⅓ cup nonfat dry milk powder
 ½ cup packed brown sugar
 1 teaspoon baking soda
 1 teaspoon cinnamon
 ½ teaspoon nutmeg
 ½ teaspoon cloves
 ½ teaspoon salt
 1 egg
 ½ cup vegetable oil
 ½ cup applesauce
 2 cups cooked green or wax beans or 1 16-ounce can green or wax beans,
    well drained
 ¾ cup chopped walnuts
 ½ cup currants
 2 tablespoons confectioners' sugar

Stir together first 8 ingredients in mixing bowl until evenly mixed.

Place egg, oil, applesauce, and beans in blender; blend smooth. Pour over dry ingredients; mix well. Stir in nuts and currants. Pour into greased 11¼ × 7½ × 1½-inch pan. Bake at 350°F 25 to 30 minutes. Sprinkle with confectioners' sugar while warm. Cut into bars.

desserts

cranberry apple crisp

Yield: 6 to 8 servings

    3 cups apple slices (5 to 6 medium apples, peeled, cored, sliced)
    2 cups whole fresh or frozen cranberries
    2 tablespoons honey
    ½ cup butter or margarine
    1 cup rolled oats
    ½ cup whole-wheat flour
    ¾ cup firmly packed brown sugar
    ½ cup chopped nuts
    ½ teaspoon vanilla

Combine apple slices and cranberries. Drizzle with honey; toss lightly to coat.

With pastry blender cut butter into oats, flour, and brown sugar; mix until crumbly. Stir in nuts and vanilla.

Place apples and cranberries in greased 11¾ × 7½-inch baking dish. Top with oat mixture. Bake at 350°F about 50 minutes or until browned and bubbly.

Serve dish warm, with whipped cream if desired.

apple–grape salad

Yield: 4 servings

> 2 medium tart apples, peeled, quartered, cored
> ½ pound blue grapes, halved, seeded
> 1 stalk garden mint (leaves only)
> 2 teaspoons sugar
> 2 tablespoons lemon juice
> 2 tablespoons brandy

Cut apples crosswise in thin slices. Arrange grapes, apples, and mint leaves in glass bowl. Sprinkle with sugar, lemon juice, and brandy. Toss lightly; cover. Chill 1 hour.

apple–grape salad

126

baked apples with cranberry filling

baked apples with cranberry filling

Yield: 4 servings

    4 large apples, cores removed to ½ inch of bottoms
    8 tablespoons whole cranberry sauce
    1 tablespoon butter or margarine
    ¾ cup boiling water
    2 tablespoons sugar

Fill centers of apples with cranberry sauce. Dot tops with butter. Place in 8 × 8-inch pan with ¾ cup boiling water. Bake in preheated 375°F oven 40 to 60 minutes or until tender but not mushy.

Serve apples hot or cold. Sprinkle with sugar just before serving.

cranberry applesauce

Yield: 2½ to 3 quarts

    5 pounds red apples (about 25 apples)
    ¾ cup water
    1 pound cranberries
    1¼ cups sugar, more or less, depending on sweetness of apples

Wash apples; cut into quarters. (Do not peel or core.) Place water and quartered apples in large Dutch oven (5- or 6-quart size).

Wash cranberries; place on top of apples. Cover; bring to boil over medium heat. Lower heat; cook until apples lose their shape and are tender, about ½ hour. Stir occasionally to prevent sticking and to allow apples to cook uniformly. When apples and cranberries are cooked, remove from heat; press through food mill. Sweeten with sugar to taste.

Serve applesauce warm or chilled. Extra applesauce can be frozen or canned.

ambrosia

Yield: 6 to 8 servings

>3 oranges, peeled, sectioned
>2 bananas, peeled, sliced diagonally
>½ teaspoon lemon juice
>2 cups strawberries, washed, hulled
>1 small cantaloupe, peeled, seeded, sliced
>1 papaya, peeled, seeded, sliced (optional)
>½ cup flaked coconut

Sprinkle lemon juice on bananas to prevent darkening. Arrange fruits in individual serving dishes. Sprinkle coconut over tops.

peanutty snack bananas

Children love these peanutty bananas for after-school snacks, but they are equally delicious for a quick-and-easy family dessert.

Yield: 1 banana makes 8 snacks

>Bananas
>Peanut butter
>Granola

Split peeled bananas lengthwise. Spread halves with peanut butter. Cut each slice into quarters. Sprinkle with granola.

pineapple–grape parfaits

Yield: 6 servings

>2½ cups halved seedless green grapes
>1 8-ounce can (1 cup) crushed pineapple, drained
>¼ cup brown sugar
>Dash of ginger
>1 cup sour cream
>¾ cup chopped walnuts

Reserve 6 grape halves for topping. Combine grapes and pineapple.
Stir brown sugar and ginger into sour cream in separate bowl.
Alternately spoon fruit mixture and sour-cream mixture into 6 parfait glasses, starting with fruit and ending with sour cream. Equally divide walnuts on top of each parfait. Place reserved grape halves over nuts. Chill several hours before serving.

fruit with honey sauce

Yield: 4 servings

  2 peaches, peeled, cubed
  2 cups fresh or canned pineapple chunks
  2 apples, peeled, cored, cut into rings
  1 cup water or pineapple juice
  ⅓ cup honey
  1 thin lemon slice
  1 stick cinnamon
  1 banana, sliced lengthwise and in half
  2 tablespoons sliced almonds
  Whipped cream for garnish
  4 cherries or grapes

Combine all ingredients, except last 4, in small casserole. Cover; cook at 350°F 40 minutes. Add banana; just heat through.

Serve fruit warm. Garnish each serving with almonds, whipped cream, and a cherry or grape.

fruit with honey sauce

apple biscuit dessert

Yield: 5 to 6 servings

brown-sugar syrup

> 1 cup water
> ½ cup packed brown sugar
> 2 tablespoons butter or margarine

Combine ingredients in small saucepan; bring to boil. Boil 2 minutes; set aside.

apple mixture

> 4 cups chopped apples, peeled, cored (6 to 7 medium apples)
> ⅔ cup packed brown sugar
> ½ teaspoon cinnamon

Prepare apples. Combine brown sugar and cinnamon. Set aside while preparing biscuit dough.

biscuit dough

> 1 cup whole-wheat pastry flour
> 1 cup all-purpose flour
> 1 tablespoon baking powder
> ¾ teaspoon salt
> ⅔ cup milk
> ⅓ cup vegetable oil
> 1 egg, beaten

Stir together flours, baking powder, and salt.
Beat together milk, oil, and egg.
Pour wet ingredients over dry ingredients; stir lightly just until thoroughly moistened. Spread half of dough in greased shallow 2-quart baking dish.
Spread dough with chopped apples. Sprinkle with cinnamon–sugar mixture. Drop remaining dough by small spoonfuls over apples and sugar, to cover top. (Top does not need to be solidly covered.) Pour syrup over all. Bake at 375°F about 50 minutes, until golden brown.
Serve dessert warm with whipped cream.

pear dumplings with honey custard sauce

Yield: 6 servings

honey custard sauce

> 1¾ cups milk
> 4 egg yolks, beaten
> 3 tablespoons honey
> 1 teaspoon vanilla
> Salt to taste

Heat milk until bubbles appear around edges.

Blend together egg yolks and honey.

Stirring, add small amount hot milk to egg yolks. Slowly return mixture to hot milk in pan, stirring continuously. Cook over hot water in top of double boiler until mixture coats spoon; continue stirring. Remove from heat. Stir in vanilla and salt; chill.

dumplings

> 2 cups whole-wheat pastry flour
> ¾ teaspoon salt
> ¼ teaspoon nutmeg
> ½ cup butter or margarine
> 4 to 6 tablespoons cold water
> 6 ripe firm pears
> 2 tablespoons lemon juice
> ⅓ cup brown sugar
> ¾ teaspoon cinnamon

Stir together flour, salt, and nutmeg. Cut butter into flour mixture until size of peas. Add water, small amount at a time, until mixture holds together. Divide pastry into 6 balls.

Peel pears; do not remove stems. Brush each with lemon juice; roll in mixture of brown sugar and cinnamon.

Roll each dough ball into 7-inch circle. Place center of each pastry over stem of each pear, letting stem pierce pastry. Mold dough around pears with hands, bringing edges together at bottom. Press edges together to seal. Place upright in greased shallow baking pan. Bake at 400°F 45 to 50 minutes or until pear is tender when pierced with fork.

Serve warm, topped with cold Honey Custard Sauce. Sprinkle with extra nutmeg if desired.

granola doughnuts

Yield: 24 to 30 bite-size doughnuts

1 cup all-purpose flour
½ cup whole-wheat flour
¾ cup sugar
1 teaspoon salt
1½ teaspoons baking powder
1 teaspoon nutmeg
1 egg, beaten

½ cup milk
¼ cup vegetable oil
½ cup Granola (see Index)
½ cup raisins
Oil for frying (oil should be at least 2 inches
    deep in fryer or saucepan)
1 teaspoon cinnamon

Sift together flours, ¼ cup sugar, salt, baking powder, and nutmeg. Add egg, milk, and ¼ cup oil; beat until smooth. Stir in Granola and raisins.

Heat frying oil to 375°F. Drop batter by teaspoonfuls into hot oil. Cook only about 6 doughnuts at a time to prevent oil from cooling down. Fry doughnuts 1½ to 2 minutes or until light brown. Turn doughnuts when bottoms are brown. Drain on paper towels.

Place ½ cup sugar and cinnamon in paper bag; shake to combine. Place drained doughnuts in bag; shake to coat doughnuts on all sides. Remove doughnuts from bag; cool on racks.

granola doughnuts

fresh apple and raisin cake

Yield: 9 × 13-inch cake

1¼ cups all-purpose flour
1 cup whole-wheat flour
2 cups sugar
2 teaspoons baking soda
1 teaspoon salt
1 teaspoon cinnamon
½ teaspoon cloves
½ teaspoon nutmeg
¼ teaspoon allspice
½ cup shortening, room temperature
⅓ cup chopped walnuts
½ cup raisins (soften in warm water if dry; drain)
2 eggs, beaten
4 cups chopped, peeled apples

Sift dry ingredients together into large mixing bowl. Add remaining ingredients; beat by hand or with electric mixer until well blended. Turn batter into greased and floured 9 × 13 × 2-inch pan. Bake at 350°F about 45 minutes or until done. Cool; frost in pan with Penuche Frosting (recipe follows).

penuche frosting

Yield: Covers 9 × 13-inch cake

¼ cup butter or margarine
½ cup brown sugar
2 tablespoons milk
1½ cups confectioners' sugar
½ teaspoon vanilla

Melt butter; add brown sugar and milk. Heat to boiling; cook 1 minute. Cool to lukewarm. Beat in confectioners' sugar and vanilla. Add more confectioners' sugar if necessary for good spreading consistency. Frost cake.

carrot cake

Yield: 10-inch bundt cake

3 eggs, separated
½ cup brown sugar
½ cup sugar
½ cup vegetable oil
2½ teaspoons vanilla
1½ cups whole-wheat pastry flour
1 cup all-purpose flour
2 teaspoons baking soda
½ teaspoon baking powder
½ teaspoon salt
1½ teaspoons cinnamon
¼ teaspoon clove
½ cup milk
2½ cups grated carrots
½ cup grated coconut
½ cup chopped nuts

Beat together egg yolks and sugars. Blend in oil and vanilla. Set aside.

Stir together flours, soda, baking powder, salt, cinnamon, and clove. Add flour mixture to sugar mixture alternately with milk; stir well. Blend in carrots, coconut, and nuts.

Beat egg whites until stiff but not dry. Fold into cake batter just until evenly distributed. Pour into well-greased 10-inch bundt pan. Bake at 350°F 40 to 45 minutes or until cake tests done. Let cool 10 minutes. Remove from pan to rack to finish cooling.

Just before serving, sprinkle with powdered sugar if desired.

chocolate oatmeal cake

Yield: 8-inch-square cake

⅔ cup boiling water
½ cup rolled oats
¼ cup butter or margarine
½ cup packed brown sugar
⅓ cup sugar
¾ teaspoon vanilla
1 egg, beaten
¾ cup whole-wheat pastry flour
½ teaspoon baking powder
½ teaspoon baking soda
¼ teaspoon salt
2 tablespoons cocoa

Pour boiling water over oats. Let stand 15 to 20 minutes.

Cream together butter and sugars. Beat in vanilla and egg. Add oatmeal; beat well.

Stir together flour, baking powder, soda, salt, and cocoa. Add to oatmeal mixture; stir until well blended. Pour into greased 8-inch-square baking pan. Bake at 350°F 25 to 30 minutes or until done.

Serve cake plain, with whipped cream, or sprinkled with confectioners' sugar.

chocolate–nut kuchen

Yield: 8½ × 4½-inch loaf

1 cup whole-wheat flour
1½ cups all-purpose flour
1 teaspoon salt
1 teaspoon baking soda
½ cup honey
¼ cup butter or margarine, softened
1 egg, beaten
⅔ cup milk
½ cup chopped walnuts or hazelnuts
½ cup raisins (optional)
1 6-ounce package semisweet chocolate chips

Sift flours, salt, and baking soda together.
Cream honey and butter.
Combine egg and milk.
Add dry ingredients alternately with egg–milk mixture to honey butter. Stir in nuts and raisins. Pour batter into greased loaf pan. Bake at 350°F about 60 minutes or until done. Remove loaf from pan to cool.
Melt chocolate chips. Brush top of loaf with melted chocolate. Cool; serve.

chocolate–nut kuchen

prune oatmeal cake

Yield: 9 × 13-inch cake

1¼ cups boiling water
1 cup rolled oats
½ cup butter or margarine
1 cup packed brown sugar
¾ cup white sugar
2 eggs, beaten
1½ teaspoons vanilla

1½ cups whole-wheat pastry flour
1 teaspoon baking powder
1 teaspoon baking soda
½ teaspoon salt
¾ teaspoon cinnamon
¼ teaspoon nutmeg
1 cup pitted prunes, chopped

Pour boiling water over oats. Let stand 20 minutes.

Meanwhile cream together butter and sugars. Add eggs and vanilla; beat until light and fluffy.

Stir together flour, baking powder, soda, salt, cinnamon, and nutmeg.

Stir oat mixture into butter and sugar. Add flour mixture; blend until well mixed. Stir in prunes. Pour into greased 9 × 13-inch baking pan. Bake at 350°F 25 to 30 minutes, until toothpick inserted in center comes out clean. Remove from oven. Spread topping on hot cake. Broil 2 to 4 minutes, until coconut is golden brown. Watch carefully while mixture is broiling. Cool; cut into squares.

topping

½ cup brown sugar
½ cup chopped walnuts
1 cup shredded coconut
⅓ cup butter or margarine, melted
¼ cup milk or light cream

Just before cake is done, combine all ingredients, ready to spread on warm cake.

whole-wheat single pie crust

Yield: 1-crust pie shell

½ cup all-purpose flour
½ cup whole-wheat flour
½ teaspoon salt
¼ cup shortening
3 tablespoons cold water

Sift flours and salt together. Cut in shortening with two knives or pastry blender. Add 2 tablespoons cold water. Stir with fork until dough begins to stick together. Add more water if needed. Form dough into ball. Let rest 10 minutes. Roll out dough between waxed paper; fit into quiche or pie pan. Depending on use, bake at 400°F 12 minutes or partially bake at 400°F 7 minutes.

whole-wheat double pie crust

Yield: Double crust for 9-inch pie

   2 cups whole-wheat pastry flour
   ½ teaspoon salt
   ½ cup vegetable oil
   ¼ cup water

Stir together flour and salt.

Combine oil and water. Pour over flour. Stir with fork until moistened. Shape into 2 balls, using hands. Roll each ball between pieces of waxed paper. Remove top waxed paper. Invert over pie plate; gently peel second paper from dough. Pat together any cracks or tears.

Prick top crust with fork after it is in place over filling.

yogurt apple pie

Yield: 6 servings

   ½ cup sugar
   2½ tablespoons all-purpose flour
   ½ teaspoon cinnamon
   Dash of nutmeg
   4 cups peeled and sliced apples
   1 egg, beaten
   1 cup plain yogurt
   ½ teaspoon vanilla
   ½ teaspoon almond extract
   1 9-inch Whole-Wheat Pastry Crust, unbaked (see Index)

Combine sugar, flour, cinnamon, and nutmeg with apples in large mixing bowl; set aside.

Mix together egg, yogurt, vanilla, and almond extract. Fold yogurt mixture into apples until well blended. Pour into pie shell. Spoon topping over yogurt–apple mixture. Bake 40 to 45 minutes at 400°F.

topping

   ¼ cup butter or margarine
   ¼ cup brown sugar
   ¼ cup whole-wheat flour
   2 tablespoons toasted wheat germ
   ½ cup chopped walnuts

With pastry blender, crumble butter, sugar, flour, and wheat germ until size of peas. Stir in walnuts.

cranberry mince pie

Yield: 9-inch pie

1 9-ounce package condensed mincemeat
2 cups coarsely chopped cranberries
2 cups water
½ cup sugar
¼ teaspoon vanilla
Pastry for 9-inch Double Pie Crust (see Index)
⅓ cup chopped walnuts
2 teaspoons butter or margarine

Crumble mincemeat. Combine with cranberries in medium saucepan. Add water and sugar. Stirring, bring to boil over medium heat. Cook and stir 4 to 5 minutes, until mixture thickens somewhat and cranberries are partially cooked. Cool; add vanilla. Pour into unbaked pie crust. Sprinkle with chopped nuts. Dot with butter. Add top crust. Bake at 400°F 40 minutes or until done.

prune nut pie

Yield: 9-inch pie

3 eggs, beaten
1 cup light corn syrup
½ cup sugar
1 teaspoon vanilla
¼ teaspoon salt
2 cups chopped pitted prunes
½ cup walnuts, coarsely chopped
1 9-inch unbaked Single Pie Crust (see Index)

Combine eggs, corn syrup, sugar, vanilla, and salt. Stir in prunes and nuts. Pour into pie shell. Bake at 350°F 45 to 50 minutes or until knife inserted comes out clean. Let cool.
Serve pie with whipped cream if desired.

blancmange

Yield: 4 servings

3 tablespoons cornstarch	¼ cup cold milk
⅓ cup sugar	2 cups hot milk
¼ teaspoon salt	1 teaspoon vanilla

Mix cornstarch, sugar, and salt in top of double boiler. Add cold milk; stir until smooth. Add hot milk gradually; cook 15 minutes, stirring constantly, until mixture thickens. Add flavoring; chill.

baked caramel custard

Yield: 4 servings

> 1 cup sugar
> ¼ cup water
> 1 4- to 6-cup metal mold
> 4 eggs
> 2 egg yolks
> 2½ cups hot milk
> Dash of salt
> 1 teaspoon vanilla

Put ½ cup sugar and water into mold. Heat until sugar caramelizes and turns dark brown. Immediately dip mold into pan of cold water 2 to 3 seconds to cool. Tilt pan so mixture films bottom and sides of mold with caramel.

Combine eggs, yolks, and ½ cup sugar in medium-size bowl; beat until well-mixed and foamy. Stir in 1¼ cups hot milk; mix well. Add remaining milk, salt, and vanilla; stir well. Strain sauce through sieve to remove coagulated egg. Pour into mold. Skim off foam on top.

Preheat oven to 325°F.

Set mold in larger pan. Pour boiling water around mold to come halfway up its sides. Place on lowest oven rack. Bake custard 45 minutes or until center is firm. Cool, then refrigerate custard.

When ready to unmold, run knife around edge; set in lukewarm water 1 or 2 minutes. Place serving plate upside down over mold; quickly invert.

vermont maple–apple pudding

Yield: 4 to 6 servings

> 6 tablespoons butter or margarine
> ¼ cup packed brown sugar
> 1 cup whole-wheat pastry flour
> 2½ teaspoons baking powder
> ¼ teaspoon salt
> ½ teaspoon cinnamon
> 1 cup milk
> ½ cup pure maple syrup
> ½ teaspoon vanilla
> 3 medium apples, peeled, coarsely chopped (2 cups)

Melt butter in 2-quart casserole dish.

Stir together brown sugar, flour, baking powder, salt, and cinnamon.

Combine milk, maple syrup, and vanilla. Pour over flour mixture; blend until smooth. Pour batter over melted butter in casserole; do not stir. Place apples on top of batter. Bake in 375°F oven 35 to 40 minutes, until crust turns brown.

Serve pudding warm with plain cream.

tapioca stewed fruit

Try baking this fragrant dessert on a cold winter day with an "all-oven" meal.

Yield: 6 to 8 servings

¼ cup pearl tapioca
⅔ cup water
1 8-ounce package mixed dried fruit or 8 ounces dried peaches, apricots, and
    pears, mixed
½ cup dried apples, coarsely chopped
½ cup pitted prunes, coarsely chopped
¼ cup currants
¼ cup chopped cranberries
2 cups water
2 cups apricot nectar
½ cup packed brown sugar
½ orange, sliced thinly, seeds removed
½ lemon, sliced thinly, seeds removed
1 cinnamon stick

Soak pearl tapioca in water overnight.
Add remaining ingredients. Pour into 3-quart casserole or Dutch oven; cover.
Bake at 350°F 65 to 75 minutes, until thickened and fruit is soft. Remove from oven;
let set until cool enough to eat. Remove cinnamon stick.
Serve warm, or refrigerate and serve cold.

golden pearl tapioca

Yield: 4 to 5 servings

½ cup pearl tapioca
Water to cover
2 cups warm water
¾ cup nonfat dry milk powder
1 stick cinnamon

⅓ cup packed brown sugar
2 eggs, beaten
½ teaspoon salt
1 teaspoon vanilla

Soak tapioca overnight in water to cover.
Drain tapioca. Place in top of double boiler. Add warm water, dry milk, and
cinnamon stick. Cook over low heat, stirring occasionally, about 50 minutes or until
tapioca is clear.
Beat together sugar, eggs, and salt.
When tapioca has finished cooking, remove cinnamon stick. Add small amount
hot tapioca to egg mixture, then gradually stir egg mixture into tapioca. Cook, stirring, about 5 minutes, but *do not let boil*. Remove from heat. Add vanilla.
Spoon tapioca into dishes. Serve warm or chilled. Cooled mixture will be
thicker.

beverages

frozen lemonade mix

Yield: 6 servings

1 teaspoon freshly grated lemon peel
¾ cup sugar

½ cup boiling water
1 cup freshly squeezed lemon juice

Combine peel, sugar, and boiling water in quart freezer container. Stir until sugar is dissolved. Add lemon juice. Cover; freeze until needed.

To make lemonade, add 5 cups water; stir. Add ice cubes.

apple–pineapple cooler

Yield: 1½ quarts

3 cups unsweetened apple juice
2 cups unsweetened pineapple juice
1 cup orange juice
2 tablespoons freshly squeezed lime
 or lemon juice
Orange slices to garnish

Combine ingredients; chill. Garnish glasses with orange slices.

fruit tea punch

Yield: About 10 cups

2 cups boiling water
4 black-tea bags
¼ cup lemon juice
2 cups orange juice
1 tablespoon honey
1 lemon
2 oranges
2 cups fresh strawberries
1 bottle soda water

fruit tea punch

Pour boiling water over tea bags. Steep 3 minutes; remove tea bags. Blend in lemon and orange juice; sweeten with honey.

Cut peel from lemon and oranges; section fruit. Remove all membranes. Add to tea.

Wash and hull strawberries; cut in half; add to tea. Cover; refrigerate punch at least 6 hours to blend flavors.

Just before serving, add bottle of soda water.

141

index

144